Karl-Heinz Hermsch

The disenchantment of consciousness

(Revised edition)

© Karl-Heinz Hermsch 2023

Version: January 2026

1

Preliminary remark

There are, among others,

4 types, something consider.

(E.g. the content of a Non-fiction):

> 1. One cannot understand that.
>
> 2. You don't want to understand that because it doesn't fit your own worldview. *(So, not to the aims that created this.)*
>
> 3. You use your cognitive abilities to understand it.
>
> 4. One has judged beforehand and thinks one understands everything.

Contents

Starting point

<u>Consciousness is a term from philosophy that could never be defined exactly and therefore always remained vague.</u>

The reason for this is that philosophers generally did not want to accept that life arose from matter; that it naturally also follows substances and laws.

They want to see in man a being that, beyond the material, has metaphysical states, experiences, and a free will, especially with its 'consciousness'.

These are wishes that cannot be fulfilled with the facts, with reality – but are possible with the mid-point - mechanism. In other words: this blind them; thus, fulfils their illusions.

A clear, real definition of *consciousness* is obtained when it is described with **increased attention** (the function of which is to look at something

more closely). This avoids the sublimi-
nal reference to metaphysics.

It is created by the senses (the sensory system*) when certain thresholds are exceeded. These of course immediately activate all the affected neural networks in order to be able to react.

(*Sensory systems are the recording of environmental stimuli and body states and their forwarding.)

This increased attention cannot make a decision on its own due to a lack of information. The human mind (as an information seeker in the neural networks) can only contribute partial information through its activities.

Ultimately, decisions are: concerted results from many neural networks <u>in order to achieve aims</u>.

The belief that we control ourselves with our consciousness is rarely questioned because this is how it has been handed down and feeling imposes this with apparent evidence.

So, we usually experience ourselves as a person in whom it makes all decisions.

The brain is seen as an aid: as the bearer of memory. It is also recognized that inherited traits and learned skills are stored here.

It is often less clear that it also regulates all feelings, thinking, actions, etc.

If you look more closely, you can see that the brain controls us, in which the ego (i.e. its aims) is also located. This is an essential ally and decision-maker.

(For normal, daily life, however, it is usually irrelevant to know that the brain controls you: you act and react to events that are important to you.)

But it can be interesting for anyone who wants to know why consciousness exists:

1. The brain shows us the world according to its aims. (It is generally known that it selects the world.

2. General attention sees it in this form plus what the sensory system also picks up.

3. It sends this modified image back to the brain. If it decides that it is important (for example because essential similarities are missing), increased attention is generated in the senses.

4. These then show us the world, which may have changed - and store it.

5. The increased attention now sees it in this form plus what the senses then pick up.

6. It sends this information back to the brain.

7. etc.

These sequences repeat themselves constantly every millisecond. Depending on the value, with normal attention or with increased senses.

So: **What you see first is first made exclusively by the brain, which shows it to us based on its aims.** Then what the sensory system experiences is sent to the brain, which processes it. And then shows the attention a corrected view, depending on the deviation.

Therefore, it is only perceived milliseconds after the brain has made the decision.

Because the brain always decides - because it has countless pieces of information in it - based on its aims. Consciousness never decides because it only experiences and is very limited in terms of what it can simultaneously absorb from the brain.

And only with sufficient information can appropriate decisions be made.

This makes it very clear: Consciousness or normal attention cannot interpret the world suffi-

ciently to make decisions because this is the domain of the brain; it does not have its information.

The brain cannot experience the present clearly enough without information from the sensory system. It needs it in order to possibly correct its interpretation of the world and decide differently.

In summary:

> *The senses experience the world according to the specifications of the aims and send different results to the neural networks.*
>
> *This is then recorded and processed in the brain.*

Of course, consciousness does not decide. **The brain decides** according to the aims and information it contains.

If it does not receive current information from outside, it can of course only judge based on what is inside it.

Ultimately, it is about perception. Either the normal, more general kind (such as moving through a familiar environment). Or an attentive, conscious kind, through the amplification of the senses (e.g. when you are in an unfamiliar area).

Perception therefore has the task of giving the brain information through experience. This may generate new learning processes, make corrections, change settings, activate aims, etc.

The brain draws up suggestions, anticipates or rejects them, i.e. anticipates results - which are experienced by perception and transmits the resulting perspectives and information back to the brain.

If something is currently important to us, if something dangerous, unusual or new occurs, if decisions or activities of the neural networks exceed a certain threshold in the brain, it amplifies our senses. This means that we perceive the outside and inside world more intensely. We experience it more vividly.

The amplified senses (through perception) then send the information they have received to the brain - especially to the neural networks affected by it, which (largely with their feelings) may make a change in assessment and attitude. This result is perceived again, etc.

The feeling offers solutions to an issue based on similar events in the past.

If you decide on a different solution, perhaps because you have paid more attention to the current issue, then you can get a bad gut feeling.

This arises because you did not accept the decision regarding another, similar situation.

(It occurs (as mentioned) due to similar events in the past. Of course, it does not prove with irrefutable facts that a different decision regarding the current situation is wrong, because the two are usually not the same.)

Prologue

> **Consciousness is nothing supernatural, just perception.**
>
> **It is gained by concentrating on an aim that opens the relevant midpoint (neuronal network).**

When asked what consciousness is, the answer is often:

Consciousness is the perception of the brain with which the SELF can make its decisions.

This raises two questions:

1. How is it perceived?

2. What is the SELF?

Wikipedia*: Perception in living beings is the process and the **subjective result** of information acquisition (reception) and processing of stimuli from the environment and from within the body. This happens through unconscious (and sometimes conscious in humans) filtering and merging of partial information into subjectively meaningful overall impressions. These are also called precepts and are continuously compared with stored ideas (constructs and schemes).*

To 1: In order to be able to subjectively filter, **aims are required** that lead to the acquisition of information.

To 2: Here, too, it is the **aims** of the respective person that he wants to achieve.

▶ Definition:

> **The SELF is initially formed from feelings: what do I like, what do I dislike. Over time these changes to: I want that, I don't want that.**

So, in all cases they are aims.

▶ Definition:

> **Human drives are the aims in the brain.**
>
> **Which, like everything in the universe, proceed according to laws.**

How did they come up?

They arose through heredity and in the course of life and formed neural networks in the brain.

The question of how the stimuli from the environment are absorbed is obvious: **by the senses**. A selection already takes place here; because it is impossible to absorb all the stimuli that surround people and are constantly changing.

Wikipedia: The filtering of stimuli is the central prerequisite for survival in their environment for all animals, but to a certain extent also for unicellular organisms and plants. Every living being constantly receives significantly more stimuli than the potential sensory cells or cell components and the cells downstream from them (cell components) could process.

That means: At this fundamental level, a selection takes place through the **aims** in the person that are important to him. He (mostly unconsciously) directs his attention to these.

**So, you always come across
aims that shape people.**

In relation to one another, one
notices little of what normal attention picks up. The information through the senses (of
the sensors) is usually unconscious. But as soon as something is very important, the attention is focused more on it.

**And this is exactly where
consciousness takes place!**

▶ **Definition:**

> ***Consciousness*** **is in-
> creased perception of
> the sensory system (tak-
> ing in environmental
> stimuli and body states**

and passing them on) that exceed certain thresholds.

► Since there is also no clear definition of the psyche on the part of the experts, I suggest this:

The psyche consists of the neural networks in the brain.

At this point it is fundamental to make my term **"midpoint"** clear which shapes the psyche.

In each case, it describes a neural network that is developed by an aim in order to achieve it.

The more the brain pursues an aim, the less other aims cannot contribute to it are perceived or can work.

This is the general brain knitting pattern. (See the chapter Midpoint-Mechanics in this book).

▶ And finally: textbooks unfortunately do not teach the central motifs of living beings:

Human drives are the aims in the brain.

It struck me that it is diffi-cult for many psychologists (and philosophers) to under-stand <u>that people are guided by neural networks</u>. They still assume that they control themselves with their con-sciousness, which should al-so be their SELF.

This attitude can be de-scribed as "dogmatic veil".

There is a tendency for a number of academics not to be sceptical about their own theory.

The term dogmatism denotes the attitude that there are certain incontestable, secure opinions and statements.

This is particularly true of the expression "human mind", which is also spangly called a mental state; it is meant to represent something intangible.

Among other things, he comes from the field of metaphysics, whose foundations are faith and speculation, with the aim of representing man as something that should also represent him as a creature of a non-physical world.

Ultimately, this has been produced without sufficient evidence by people expressing their wishful thinking.

Often associated with this attitude is the notion that these do not have to be proven.

Dogmatism defies any criticism and holds – whatever others say, whatever developments may be going on – unwaveringly clinging to the possibly correct sensations.

And: their representatives are often not aware of being dogmatists.

The behaviour of these people today is similar to that of the past with the Copernican system: the midpoint, the geocentric worldview - the earth is in the center of the universe - prevented insight into the heliocentric worldview: the earth is merely a planet that is itself moved around the sun. The leading intellectual class at that time could not and did not want to break away from these ideas contained in them, the geocentric worldview.

It only went out in the following generations.

The current view of consciousness is similar. This is not something that makes decisions and directs the brain, but it is controlled by the brain, which activates the senses accordingly through the respective aims, so that the consciousness experiences with strengthened senses and provides further information.

A quick note about our senses:

> **The brain can only perceive the world through the senses.**
>
> **So, the senses create the connections to the world - however, the vision is limited by the brain with its aims right from the start.**
>
> **That is, they do not take in the world as a whole, but only what is essential for the aims in the brain.**
>
> **This saves time and is more economical than if the senses were to absorb everything**

first (which would not even
be possible).

Conclusion:

The general or conscious attention sends the recorded information to the neural networks, which process it. These change, if they are relevant, attitudes, behaviour etc.

The outdated attitude towards consciousness, with which the mind knows everything and

then makes decisions
with its ego, can no
longer be maintained.

No one has yet been able
to define the functions
of this consciousness.

However, this is possi-
ble without contradic-
tion with the postulate
of the aims through
which neural networks
are formed.

> In this book you can read carefully researched new perspectives.
>
> It's a treasure chest of fresh inspiration.

Constructive criticism is welcome.

> "CP" represents countless conversations partner with whom I have discussed the topics for many years.

Consciousness

(Conversation about)

With the topic:

> Expanding Consciousness
>
> Complex
>
> World view
>
> Feelings
>
> Control
>
> Condemnation
>
> Freedom / Determinism
>
> SELF, It, Superego

"You say Consciousness is an amplification of the senses," summarized CP.
"And you mean it doesn't make any
decisions."

"Consciousness is enhanced sensory awareness (taking in environmental stimuli and bodily states and relaying them) using a voluntary or involuntary focus to provide the most accurate information possible to targets in the brain," I nodded.

"That's a description that most people are probably unfamiliar with."

"Because they project into 'consciousness' the entire 'freedom of human beings' without examining them in detail."

"You mean, it would ultimately come out that it's just an information transmitter for the brain?" asked GP.

▶ "**Consciousness** (the heightened senses) or normal attention might not interpret the world sufficiently for decision-making because that is the domain of the brain; it neither possesses its information nor can it experience it at the necessary speed to react.
▶ **The brain** needs the information from consciousness (the senses) in order to possibly correct its interpreta-

tion of the world and to decide differently or to change its aims.

"Before we think we've made a decision, the brain has already made it milliseconds beforehand - when, as a rule, consciousness is no longer sending essential information.

It is important to know: life always also means: experiencing feelings. And that the brain is their memory, in the respective neural networks. "

"But why do you need consciousness at all, because the information from the senses could also be stored in the brain without it?"

"That is also done with normal atten-tion. But if something is important and essential, you have to look at it more closely. This is the job of conscious-ness.

Feelings in particular are eminently important because they are of outstanding importance for people with regard to aims.

As I said: the brain does not perceive. It just builds the world for us according to its aims. In other words, it takes its attention or consciousness from this perspective, experiences it with this "reality" that is then present and transfers the information to the brain.

That is why we must have attention and, in reinforcement, consciousness. "

▶ **"The world as a whole, in all parts, is not as we see it, but always like our brain, to be more precise; his aims they show us"**, **recapitulated CP.**

"Many people don't realize this," I nodded. "For them, the world is as they themselves and others (apparently also) see: the same and unambiguous.

The fact that aims in the brain shape the respective world according to our dispositions and experiences, which only human perspectives can evoke, is usually strange and unimaginable to them. So, they ignore it, stick to their old point of view. "

"So, we cannot see the world objectively*."

"Always from our subjective perspective."

> ## !! The world that shows itself to us is there first, but what a person sees of it, the brain decides according to its aims. !!

Since what is important is always conscious in order to look at and

experience it more closely, consciousness is always included.

It can only be this, however, if the midpoint in which one is currently does not devalue what is important through its aim.
(See midpoint-mechanics)

It is not uncommon for there to be differences between midpoints about what is 'important'. Especially with the SELF. What this desire can be blocked by other midpoints.

In other words, what a person perceives is decided by the aims in the brain - including what is important at the moment.

From this it follows: The senses (i.e., the consciousness) do not absorb it at all, because no aims are receptive to it, since the strong midpoint in which one is currently has temporarily reduced the value of them.

CP's eyes shone. " I understand that information is not recorded because

the brain is not receiving it at the moment - not an aim - because the current network of neurons blocks all others."

I nodded. "If it were still necessary to
prove that the consciousness is neither
free nor can it make decisions, it is
obvious here."

"There is another obstacle to understanding in the form that it is often
claimed that the inorganic, i.e., matter, cannot produce anything organic.

I would like to say: The first organic
compounds arose from inorganic substances billions of years ago. Over
time, more and more complex and
more complex forms of life with differentiated functions developed from this,
including the brain.

Here are not only atoms, etc., but in
particular also neurons, synapses, and
so on, which control the physical and
mental functions of humans.

The adaptation pressure of life generates aims. The brain forms neural networks to execute them.

Many people cannot imagine that only aims in the brain control people. They believe they control themselves (with their free will and consciousness). They cannot prove this, so it remains with a feeling that it is so and has settled.

So, they cannot perceive that in this case, the aim of their faith (this midpoint) causes it.

And: Not only the perceptions are stored, but, as I said, the resulting feelings. The stronger they are, the more intensively we have experienced them with our consciousness. "

"Consciousness is experienced, the brain reacts, controls and decides," recapitulated CP.

I nodded. "The brain shows us the world on the basis of its aims - the consciousness initially sees it from these. In the second step, however, it also experiences the possible differences between the old one from the brain and the new one, which it is now also picking up - and sends this information to the brain."

"Then, following your argumentation, the world that we see afterwards would also have to change, if it has a corresponding value."

"That's exactly how it is; we perceive it differently now.

We usually do not notice this because these changes are natural and logical for the brain. "

Let me briefly outline the process:

• The brain shows us the world according to its aims.
• Consciousness sees them in this form plus that which the senses then additionally absorb.
• It sends this information to the brain.
• This then shows us the world that may have changed due to the information.

• The consciousness then sees them in this form plus that which the senses now also absorb.
• It sends this information back to the brain.

These sequences repeat themselves constantly - in fractions of milliseconds. Depending on the value, with normal attention or with reinforced senses (consciousness).

This can be verified in experiments: What you see is initially only done by the brain. Then we experience it with our senses. This is sent to the brain which processes it. And then, depending on the deviation, shows the attention a corrected view.

Consciousness or normal attention cannot interpret the world because it does not possess all the information of the brain. This cannot experience, it needs this information of the consciousness in order to possibly correct its interpretation of the world."

"Is that the same when someone wakes up in a completely unfamiliar environment?"

"Yes. But the perception of the senses works very quickly - and sends it to the brain so that, when it is important, it adjusts in a flash, accepts this view and takes it into account when making decisions.

The central point of all living things is the preservation of life. This works best by **experiencing** it.

And these, in turn, are important information for the brain that couples and stores it with each event. Without consciousness, one could not experience this because, as I said, the brain alone cannot.

If a similar situation occurs, then the corresponding feelings are activated again.

(The danger here is, if one does not consciously perceive the current situation, that one reacts not to the now, but to the past.)

"It's about attention," CP considered.

I nodded. "Attention" means being at work. 'Consciousness' means to intensify your attention. The latter usually occurs much less.

In any case, the consciousness would not be able to conclude judgment without the brain, because the set of factors for it is much too large and variable to make decisions regarding the necessary activities and actions. It would simply be overwhelmed.

It would have to generate and control processes that are constantly taking place in the brain. "

"That would hardly be possible," agreed CP.

"But", he interjected, "it is sometimes objected that when you operate a machine, you don't have to know its functions down to the last detail. It is enough to press the right buttons. "

"Consciousness would have a lot to do there and should know **which actions** in the brain are to be activated in each case.

The brain is neither a device nor a machine, nor is it a computer. All of these comparisons are lagging because brains don't work as rigidly as those just mentioned.

The brain is a structure that organizes itself through its aims. In other words, a fabric that works according to organic laws and can change its value at lightning speed if the adaptation makes it necessary.

Therefore, these objections make no sense! They are just not properly thought out.

It follows", I continued: "The brain judges. What <u>one</u> takes in by means of the senses can, depending on the value, eventually influence the decision. Because all information can have an impact on the brain – as long as it is open and flexible* – i.e., not blocked by rigid settings or a particularly strong midpoint at the moment.

However, the brain decides to what

extent they reach according to its aims.

The better one knows its functions, values and possibilities, the more influence one may have with one's SELF and the will (which is also in the brain)."

"So, 'know yourself'?"

"Know your aims, so your psyche*.

Whoever observes himself, when he consciously picks up something, will find that his senses are strongly activated. Much stronger than if it's just about general attention.

You take in life with your senses, and when something special happens, e.g., something interesting, dangerous, emotionally moving, then you also take it up intensely with your consciousness, i.e., with heightened senses.

If people are dealing with a special topic, then they need specific information."

"The aim formed in each case may concentrate on the topic, and the consciousness (i.e., the increased perception) thus provides the brain with more precise facts," concluded CP.

"Thinking, for example," I explained.

GP raised his hand. "May I intervene briefly?"

I nodded to him.

"How do you define 'thinking?'"

"Thinking is a process that seeks to answer questions in the midpoints, i.e. neural networks. – Everything that man has inherited and experienced can be found here.

This creates the loop: question>answer>question again>answer, etc.

"The senses (here as the human mind) look for information in the external or internal world in response to a stimulus or a question and immediately send it to the brain. This looks for experiences or similarities. You become aware of these interim results again, etc. The interplay goes on until you have a coherent feeling or you can't get any further. The end product of thinking is formulated by the brain and only becomes conscious for a fraction of a second or later. "

CP considered. "What comes out, is so decided or formulated by the brain?"

"Yes, by the aim's neural network formed for this quest, making the final decision. And excludes all other non-relevant neural networks.

The reason that people believe that they have made their decision based on their consciousness lies in the very short period of time - often, as I said, it is only milliseconds - between the decision of the brain and becoming conscious (i.e., taking in with the senses).

When it comes to important issues, there is always an interplay between the brain and consciousness, because the brain has only a limited amount of current information and relies on the consciousness, as an amplifier of the senses, to add new facts if necessary."

"Only the most important things become so conscious?"

 "Yes".

 "Who decides what is important?"

"The aims with their midpoints."

"There are many people who claim that you decide everything with your consciousness," CP came back to this topic.

"It's incredible what it's supposed to mean," I said. "Once you look through the definitions, you read: knowing certain facts, remembering certain events, sum of beliefs and points of view, etc.

And synonymous words for consciousness should be: intelligence, memory, conviction.

The consciousness should also have complete access to the brain, "read out" the relevant data there and evaluate this data in order to be able to make a decision. After the decision, he would have to intervene again in the neural networks of the brain, for example to start movements that are necessary to carry out the action he has chosen.

All of this applies exactly to the brain. But once you check the consciousness what it represents of it, you search in vain. Because it was not made to carry this around with you and it cannot do it at all. "

"So, people say that they control themselves with their consciousness, because they are not observing themselves closely, because they take these views for granted. They just parrot out of habit what other people say or what they have learned. This also includes using the word consciousness without reflection. "

"That hits the nail on the head," I confirmed.

"They just take it that way."

"Yes, because they have either not yet heard the statement that man is a being guided by aims of the brain or they do not want to hear it. It interferes with their usual views of the world they want to stay in. Accordingly, they do not investigate this matter either.

If all this is too complicated for them, it would help a lot if they just say perception for consciousness."

"Is that also true for scientists?"
  "Mostly yes. Their feelings do not let them see these facts."

"Does that come from the midpoint-mechanics?"

"Yes. They are at the midpoint of their feelings.

These also generate the opinion that consciousness is something that only humans have and that they control themselves with it.

--- Expansion of consciousness ---

By the way: The expression 'expansion of consciousness' also comes from this attitude. Without being clear about it, they say: The strengthened senses should absorb more information than usual (which would probably not be wrong)."

"People who use this word," remarked CP, "probably mean a kind of spiritual, metaphysical experience."

"For sure. When they create such an aim in themself, a midpoint will form that will make them feel that way. Of course, this only happens in their brains.

And it doesn't make any sense either: consciousness is just an amplified perception of the senses. So, expanding consciousness would mean; Strengthen perception to strengthen it.

Anyway", I continued, "the experiments of Libet and others (scientific writings by Benjamin Libet 1983, Keller and Heckhausen 1990, Haggard and Eimer 1999, Miller and Trevena

2002) clearly show that, before a person made a conscious decision, the brain does this decision has already been made. So, you cannot deny that the brain is deciding and not consciousness.

One particular difficulty was that in earlier times it could not be precisely defined: Consciousness was something that was not found in the brain but, as people said, controls one's actions. Because the belief in supernatural, in this case a 'consciousness-spirit being' was widespread."

"They took consciousness as a metaphysical spirit, similar to the spirit of God, without questioning it further."

I nodded. "And unfortunately, that is still the case today.

The fact that the brain decides has been clearly demonstrated by the experiments of Libet and other scientists. The so-called "freedom of consciousness" has never been proven."

"But why do educated people still cling to their version that this decides everything?"

"It fits in well with their worldview and has always been considered a cognitive and decision-making authority. One was and is sure that the entire true world could be recognized with it.

In the past, the brain explained that the world was unique - to handle it well - and that it could be perceived and recognized by people with their consciousness. Of course, that lifted the human far beyond the animals. At the latest since the emergence of the theory of relativity and quantum mechanics and their experimental confirmation, this belief is over: The world is neither unique nor the same from every perspective.

What remains in many people is the idea of the consciousness that the decision is made, because, according to its logic, it recognizes everything. Of course, this logic excludes the brain - as a decision-maker.

But consciousness is just an important interface between the brain and the outside world," I explained. "Only with its senses - and it is an amplification of these - is it possible for the brain to receive specific information from the outside and of course also from the inside."

"So, if something is important, then the senses are reinforced and consciousness comes into play," repeated CP.

"Imagine that you have the aim of making an important decision, of choosing or pronouncing judgment on the basis of relevant facts, and you should do all of this in every single sequence with just your awareness, like many people accept.

Or let's take the language, it runs automatically. One has learned how to speak, articulate and so on. An experienced speaker, of course, does not focus on the individual points of the language, but the focus is on the topic at stake.

The speaking, the gestures, the facial expressions that one makes, all this has been learned in the course of life and is, if one speaks, expressed. Consciousness has nothing to do with it, unless you behave wrong, make mistakes, then it usually becomes active immediately and delivers appropriate information to the brain. This then attempts to bring about a correction or change in behaviour.

Imagine, you have to choose all your words only with your consciousness. For example, at a party. And now ask yourself what you are really aware of. That means: how to use your movements, how you speak, facial expressions, etc. "

"That's really impossible, you need the learned routines from the brain," CP agreed.

"Yes, the respective midpoints."

"You say only the relatively most important things come to your consciousness. But how is it when I am busy with an important topic and concentrate on it. Suddenly, something comes to my consciousness that has nothing to do with the current midpoint? "

"Well, the brain jumped from one midpoint to another because it took the attention or because the previous one might just go by itself and no longer need consciousness. Or the other midpoint seemed more important to the brain at the moment, because a question that had been in one for a long time could now be answered. This often happens with creative people. Maybe they just aroused interest in some topic.

By the way: It also occurs to me that when you've forgotten something that you just wanted, it can help sometimes to ask yourself: 'What was my aim just now?'"

"You mean you jumped to another midpoint, and is less shaped by the previous one?"

I nodded. "It's like priming*.

And in general, the following applies: A very strong concentration is only possible for a limited time, because from a certain point, due to physiological factors, it decreases. "

"And otherwise, you live without consciousness?" asked CP. "If everything works and no new facts are added?"

I smiled. "Most of the time, everything actually goes off automatically, the consciousness is almost in the standby state during this time, but is immediately active again when something important occurs. Usually, this is far less the case than you should think. In addition, the brain learns, and the new usually quickly becomes routine, so that the consciousness is then no longer needed in this intensity.

If you observe yourself, you will be able to confirm this. In everyday life, you don't usually come across something exciting new or important events.

- So, attention has the task of being 'on the job' at the respective midpoints.

- The consciousness to concentrate, if necessary, in order to convey to the brain, the information that is considered to be very relevant."

"Consciousness always becomes active with intense attention when something is very important," CP repeated.

"Yes. Depending on what the attention is focused on, this gets a value that can shape or, in other words, structure man. This is the normal attention. If something is particularly important, then one speaks of a conscious recording.

Also, at the risk of repeating myself: the purpose is to provide this strong information to the aims in the brain so that they can immediately absorb them and respond accordingly. So, consciousness is always an enhancement of the senses. "

"So, attention and consciousness each deliver information to the brain?"

"Yes, the difference is in the different valence."

"Consciousness is not active that often."

"If you observe yourself, you will be able to confirm this. In everyday life you do not usually encounter something exciting new or important events.

But here one should differentiate: Adolescents and especially children have more consciousness than adults. Consciousness in the sense of increased perception. Because the world is still new and they are gathering their experiences. But that does not necessarily mean that its perception corresponds to the facts. (Because the aims in the brain guide the perception).

Conversely, it seems that the older you are, the less you usually integrate in yourself. Experience shows that neuronal plasticity is limited. However,

this is less the case for areas that have interested people for life.
Many midpoints have become firmer over the years, but also more rigid, and unfortunately often exclude new things that seemingly do not suit them with the midpoint-mechanics.

In addition, it could be interesting: Until you are around 28 years old, the bottom-up works - the sustainable recording of information that is used to shape the value of the respective person. Then comes the bottom-down - acting with established information. (One acts from the value creation that has taken place.)
Incidentally: The content of this acquired information and values is, however, usually only marginally scientifically secured.

Consciousness awakens or generates midpoints because of important values in the brain when they are particularly touched. For example: survival, new orientation, social recognition.

Is it overwhelmed or bored, then one comes to dreams.

However, the moment you leave your habitual environment, for example, the attention or consciousness becomes more active. Because new facts or impressions are important to the brain to orient itself. Movements and pictures are preferably consciously perceived. "

"What mechanism may be behind this if you're stuck with a topic, even though you think you know the solution?" CP asked.

"It's a midpoint that blocks. For example, one has gotten bogged, and in this impasse the thoughts circle. The same mechanism works when one is ruled by anger*. Generally speaking, whenever there is a midpoint that severely restricts others. "

"That reminds me," CP said, "if you've slept on it, the solution often comes to mind the next day."

"That's because the blocking midpoint has lost value or dissolved in the meantime. We have found a distance. In sleep, amongst others the brain has the task to integrate the experiences of the day's events, to learn, and possibly to create a different view through restructuring. For this, the brain prefers to use the creativity that the midpoints of the day's events can not interfere with."

"You see things in a different light," thought CP.

"Yes, the attitude changes. In other words, the other midpoints associated with this topic have been re-evaluated or others have been added. Unless this dead-end midpoint acts in the same form. Then you have a complex, so to speak.

By the way: We all know that the brain can be mistaken when it comes to recognizing and especially feeling. Therefore, before you decide something important, you should sleep on it for a night. "
--- complexes ---

"Please explain 'complex' again."

"It's a midpoint, a neural network that is unable to adapt and offers strong resistance to attempts at change."

"Has it encapsulated himself?"

"Yes, in contrast to the midpoints, which can always be learned.

Or to the clusters. These are neural networks that carry out learned or innate processes and are adaptable - such as sucking the baby on the mother's breast, walking or tying shoes. "

A cluster is therefore a midpoint, which is responsible among other things for routines, such as movements, recurring actions, learned reactions. Can you give a graphic example? "CP asked.

"Well, about a tic - a short and uncontrollable motor contraction of individual muscles in the face - is a complex. By contrast, normal facial expressions are a cluster. "

"There are, as you said, many clusters in one - skills, learned procedures, behaviours, attitudes, etc.

Can one say: complex means encapsulated?"

"Yes, it surrounds himself with walls. His aim is to maintain certain attitudes, postures, reflexes under all circumstances, and to influence other midpoints with his peculiarity of maintaining what he has once learned in a particular situation.

There are also among others Life-complex, producer-complex, Complex to follow someone. These lie entirely in the depths of the human being. This is how he is born and they practically cannot be changed.

► **The life-complex is the drive to live as long as you can, regardless of the circumstances.**

► **The producer-complex is the mainspring to produce offspring, regardless of the environmental conditions.**

► **The Complex to follow someone is devotion to a person of importance or authority who has been given special skills and whom one trusts to the point of blindness.**

As with all complexes, there is a risk of not adapting to the changed circumstances. "

"That means," thought CP, "they are rigid and do not act like other midpoints that are flexible and play along in concert with the aims of the brain."

"Yes, they don't act like the healthy midpoints, and don't learn and thus disrupt the flexibility and adaptation of the brain. This is of course unfavourable. The outside world is constantly changing. The central point of life in general and the resulting requirement should be that man adapts to these changes.

That's usually the case. Complexities prevent this, as do prejudices*, delusions, stubbornness, intolerance*. And especially fanaticism or dogmatism. "

"This is quite common," commented CP.

"I have another question," he continued. "Apart from the obviously irrefutable fact that everything consists of substances that operate according to laws*: How can one explain that there are people who believe your view of the world is the only true one? "

"You can see that very clearly in extremists, fanatics, devout believers, people who are nailed up," I nodded.

"But also, the other 'normal' people have fixed midpoints. These are their anchors, their reference points, from which they act and evaluate the world.

Anyone who realizes that their perspective is just one of many is less in danger of being torn away from the ground by the abandonment of a midpoint.

Unfortunately, here as well, the midpoints act to diminish everything else that does not support them.

The world that we see is of course still there, even if we are no longer there. However, it would change according to the respective perception by other beings who are different from us.

Because there is no such thing as a world that is always the same.

What stays forever - no matter what perspective you look at it from - is that identical substances under identical conditions always show identical results.

Many people refuse to give up a midpoint, even if it dawns on them that it is harmful to themselves. Partly because they are afraid of losing their grip.

This fear is more justified for extremists and strict believers than for other people, because they are only made special from one or a few midpoints. This is how their world could actually fall apart.

The more midpoints in a person who can play flexibly and communicate with each other, the better it is."

"Because other midpoints can intercept the inner system?"

"Yes, especially if you have focused on not just a few midpoints in your life, but many."

"You mean, if you are not just focusing on your beliefs, your family, a loved one you are fixated on, your job, your hobby, etc. you can be at risk through these midpoints if you are fully immersed in them are not seeing anything else in the long run?"

"I think so."

"So, you do not have to give up your special midpoints?" CP asked.

"You do not need that. But one thing to watch out for is that the midpoints you love will eventually get a place in one that guarantees that others will retain their value more or less. "

"Well, that a midpoint does not become a dominant ruler."

"Yes, that's important for inner harmony."

"That reminds me of complexes we just talked about."

"Midpoints that master everything are complexes."

"So, you should try to change or dissolve them," I suggested.

"That's usually difficult. If you have recognized a complex and tried to work on it, then this meets with considerable resistance. "

"What options are there?"

"You can divide the psyche of man, that is, the midpoints in the brain, into accessible and difficult to access.

If a complex interferes with healthy behaviour, and you cannot change it yourself, it is the job of a therapist, for example, to give that complex access to change or dissolve it.

The work of the brain is usually unconscious. It becomes aware when certain thresholds are exceeded. So, when something important is in the foreground, consciousness comes into action to provide information to the midpoints involved through more intense consciousness. "

"And this information does not take the encapsulated complex?"

"These can be very resistant to change - like many aims.

However, a complex does not necessarily have to be analysed down to the smallest detail, or become aware of it, so that it can be changed. If it is a learned behaviour, it is often enough to unlearn it again.

The method, such as the fear of crossing large squares, is to cross very small squares first, which can become larger if the client feels less anxious.

With others it makes more sense, as I said, to look for the reason (which always had an aim as the cause why it was formed). In this way one can possibly create an access if the consciousness stimulates a new midpoint that can bring about changes."

"You mean," concluded CP, "the one was learned and could be unlearned again. The other has formed at some point in a lifetime and could be worked through by rediscovering or raising consciousness."

"In all cases, it's about forming a new midpoint, which is increasingly reinforced by emotions and counterbalances the complex midpoint that narrows, oppresses or torments people. And who weakens or extinguishes this through the natural course of the midpoint mechanics."

"And what about the mind or the reason?"

"They can say umpteen times: 'It is nonsense what you do or think.' As long as you have not convinced the feeling, it will hardly be of any use.

--- Feelings ---

"How about the feelings when they become aware?" CP jumped to the next topic.

"Feelings are powerful controls in humans," I explained. "They arise among other things by achieving or not achieving aims.

Reaching the path strengthens the path that one had taken to reach the aim in a similar situation. If an aim is not achieved, negative feelings are triggered, which are intended to dissuade you from taking the same path in the future. At the same time, they more or less urge you to continue pursuing the aim.

Consciousness passes this information on to the brain's aims so that they can be processed by their networks. The stronger feelings for something, the more the human being gets in this midpoint. "

"Because this midpoint is reinforced by consciousness?"

"Yes, when we, for example, hear music.

Here the Qualia problem of the philosophers is often addressed.

'Qualia' means quality, quality is 'value'. The quality of a value results from
the feelings that people feel (especially
consciously). "

"Qualia means emotional value."

"Yes, people are sensitive to music
because it creates feelings in them.
The more beautiful these are, the
more value they have for him. "

"That's how the value of music comes
from the feelings you feel," said CP.
"That's nothing new."

I nodded. "That these feelings are
triggered by a midpoint is something
new.

Many philosophers do not understand
this, because the midpoint-mechanics
are unknown to them. They say that
while the brain can perceive all sorts of

stimuli, it does not explain the enjoyment of the music we feel.

I say that this enjoyment comes from
the midpoint in which I am when I
listen to music. Of course, this network
of neurons not only absorbs the stimuli, but also wholeheartedly arouses
feelings that arise in connection with
this music. "

"The more beautiful you feel music,
the more beautiful feelings it devel-
ops," added CP.

"Yes, of course the reverse is also
true: the worse the music, the less
positive feelings will unfold."

"And if someone is completely unmusi-
cal?"

"Then he feels next to nothing in this
respect."

"So, the extent to which a Qualia can
develop depends on the people who
receive it," CP concluded. The qualia
are mutually determined by the mind
and the consciousness: From one mid-

point of the receiver, to the other by the quality of the sender."

I nodded again. "To feel holistic often means to feel a similarity*. This can be seen very well in the music: You can recognize a melody that has been stored in memory, even if it is played with other instruments. Unless the instruments do not hit the tone, that is the essence of this melody. "

"Why have so many philosophers struggled to grasp this simple mechanism for over 200 years?" Asked GP.

"Because they did not know about midpoint-mechanics, so they did not have that key to the brain, they thought of consciousness as something not ultimately comprehensible, and because feelings in their subjects were often just a minor matter. This applies especially to the followers of the philosopher Immanuel Kant, who portrayed the feelings as 'opponents of reason'.

Of course, feelings have a very high value for humans - not only in the

71

negative, but of course in a positive sense. They are strong helpers of the aims - the midpoints. They control man and are not always unreasonable. What would a person be without feelings? "

"Philosophers can come to strange conclusions," CP shook his head.

I weakened. "What happened had to happen as it happened."

--- control ---

"Why is consciousness so important to many people?" He asked again.

"Because they often believe that they would decide everything with it. They need it for the feeling that they can determine absolutely freely. They don't want to realize that the brain's purposes have judged them.

They don't even want to be aware of that because they fear that they will no longer have control over themselves."

"But do people actually have control over themselves? According to everything you have explained, the brain is infinitely diverse and decides holistically with the acute goals.

"Of course you have more or less control, because the aims of the SELF are, as I have already explained, also in the psyche and play a part in the process.

The SELF can control areas of the psyche up to certain limit thresholds and, if necessary, influence them to a greater or lesser extent with its will. In other words, overcoming other aims in his psyche via the midpoint-mechanism.
But the stronger the feelings, the more difficult it becomes.
In general, the more the feelings have the power in the aims, the more difficult it is for the mind when differences arise.
This has to explain itself - not feelings!
They run according to the laws within them, which can make it difficult for the mind to influence.

This will also have something to do with the fact that people have developed in the course of their evolution through feelings - the mind only much later.
Also because of this - and because it is much easier than trying to reason - the feeling is often preferred.

And: There are, of course, a number of midpoints that have a certain strength and cannot simply be ruled by the SELF, such as the life instinct.

So many people are subject to an exaggerated illusion of control."

"After all, one shouldn't forget: The more important a decision is, the more conscious it becomes," I repeated once more. "So because people are aware of these brain decisions every time, they think they are making decisions with their consciousness.

In addition, until the 19th century, people knew little about the brain. That changed in the 20th and especially in the 21st century with the triumph of computers. This has created non-invasive methods such as:

EEG (electroencephalography),

MRI (magnetic resonance imaging),

fMRI (functional magnetic resonance imaging),

PET (positron emission tomography)

and CT (computed tomography).

These procedures allow insight into the brain, providing facts that were previously unknown.

But the old conceptions of consciousness that have been taught for thousands of years are still in people's minds today and are difficult to change. "

--- condemnation ---

"I have a question about criminal acts," CP said. "The judiciary assumes that humans are responsible for their actions.*."

"If someone commits an act, then he is in focus of the aim during this period, and it is usually not possible for the perpetrator to stop: the aim structures people, it wants to be fulfilled."

"Can't consciousness experience the effects once the brain made the decision?"

"Then of course - but not from the point of view of the aims of the brain that currently prevail."

"And he can't watch himself? Can't he be aware of what he's doing? "

"At the moment of the crime, the midpoint of the criminal act is usually so strong that it suppresses everything else."

"It is really strange that while the brain, more precisely, the midpoint decides, people do not notice this and believe it came from consciousness - that is seen as the SELF with its 'free will'."

"This is exactly what the judges believe, because they assume, as you have rightly said, that consciousness decides everything and the will is free, and both could have prevented the act."

"But if the brain has made its decision, then the consciousness could use information to signal that this is wrong," CP tried again.

"This usually excludes the aim of the midpoint. And if so, this would only work if this information is perceived and accepted by the brain, which does not happen.

Because as I said: the perpetrator is in a focus. This mechanism controls him completely, even if only for a short time. In addition, the criminal act has set a certain process in motion that is not so easy to stop. "

"So, you couldn't express any criticism at that moment, because all other midpoints - which otherwise influence perception - hardly come into play," concluded CP.

"I agree. This possible resistance in one can hardly exist as long as one is

in the midpoint of this decision, because it ensures that one practically
does not perceive anything else. And,
as I said, it sets everything else in value to almost zero. After that you often
become aware of what you have done.
But then of course you can no longer
correct it. "

--- Freedom / Determinism ---

For a moment it was quiet between us.
Then CP continued, "Can one say: Everyone knows he has consciousness,
but hardly anyone has been able to
define it yet?"

I nodded. "Although this is actually
easy if you accept the midpoint-
mechanics and are not totally absorbed by your fixed ideas: **Consciousness is intensive perception
with your senses, holistically or in
detail.**

Consciousness is also about the issue
of man's spiritual freedom. If it turns
out that everything runs according to
substances and laws*, then everything
would be predetermined, then man

would have quasi no freedom and the free will would not be there then - from the legal and philosophical point of view."

"And - is that right?" asked CP.

"The will is of course still there and plays an important role in the life of man. Will means to form a particularly strong aims for the SELF, which is also in the brain.

And human freedom would continue - because he does not know everything. And who does not know everything, is forced to make decisions. **This igno-rance is his freedom**, which man will not lose because he can never know everything.

But consciousness and **free will** in the previous sense would have to be given up.

And in the end, the fact is that every-thing is made up of substances that run according to laws and, as a result, everything is predetermined. "

"You do not mean the freedom that comes from nowhere, but the freedom of the possibilities one has. Is that ultimately freedom?" asked CP.

"It's a quasi-freedom," I answered. It is definitely a mistake to believe that there is a freedom that comes from nothing or an incomprehensible mind."

One more remark on the "spirit": A spirit, in the sense of an immaterial being, which our ancestors had felt internally and then projected outwards, because the functions of the brain - also with regard to the mid-point mechanics - were completely unknown to them only exist in humans. Everything else is projections that have no substance whatsoever in reality.

The spirits in one self are the mid-points.

They can arise and fade, in the respective context with regard to a certain value they more or less play along and shape people.

> Midpoints have the ability to suddenly show people a world that is completely different from what they are used to.

--- ego, it, superego ---

CP thought about it and then said: "There are also a lot of theories about what happens psychologically in people."

"You could say so. I would like to give an example: **An attempt was made to divide the psyche (that is, the totality of aims and their midpoints in humans**, which work via neuronal networks. For example, into SELF, It, Super-SELF, how Sigmund Freud did it.

He wrote: "The psychoanalytic" drive "is the basis of all expressions of life - regardless of the differentiated level."

If he had said aims instead of instinct, he would have come very close to the truth. Urges also play their part, of course, but are ultimately just aims. And reducing everything to urges does not lead to the reality of the psyche.

So, this does not go to the core of reality.

This is that the entire brain (which also includes the so-called abdominal brain) is a dynamic system in which the midpoints all communicate with one another more or less - and depending on the respective topic.

If one divides the psyche with three terms (self, ego, super-ego) and understands these as separate areas, it is problematic as an explanation of the soul and useless for the diagnosis of the complicated psychic processes.

Each individual component of these terms has not only developed from aims into a neural network that is located in the brain, but also correlates, mostly unconsciously, with others.

So there are not three big areas in the psyche, but a multitude of aims (midpoints) that are connected to each other:

In every living being there is a spectrum of aims that relate, detach, connect with one another, form groups

82

that act together, overlap, struggle for supremacy and arrange themselves in a sometimes-alternating hierarchy. Aims are added, others change or erase. Every aim has or creates its opponent when other aims are touched by it and run the risk of being impaired. And every action takes place through a bundle of aims that develop structures, compromise, strengthen or weaken. Many aims change in the course of life, except for the very deep ones, e.g., the life instinct. As a rule, this always remains, even if you are very old.

In this living space the behaviours are formed: actions, planning, acting, etc., the drive of instincts, and the feelings of conscience.

These are not delimited, but are subject, among other things, to the laws of midpoint-mechanics.

▶In this example, the 'ego' should be the consciousness that intervenes regulatively in the processes of the psyche.

In addition, it has the task of observing social norms, values, obedience and morality.
One can say that the consciousness only supplies the brain with information that it has received through intensive perception and that is then more or less processed by the respective midpoints - which was not known earlier. The ego is represented with its aims and midpoints in the brain and these can possibly intervene in the processes of the psyche (if it allows it) to regulate.

And as I said: **Consciousness is not the Self.**

> ▶The 'it' in this case is intended to represent the unconscious, whose content are the instincts, needs and affects.

It can be said that what one is unconscious of involves much more than these three areas, namely, among other things, procedures, communication attitudes, adaptation to the respective environment, etc.

It is also not the case that this must necessarily remain unconscious, but all these actions become conscious when they exceed a certain threshold value.

> ▶Finally, the 'super-ego' represents in the model the morality, the social norms and the conscience, which is supposed to intervene in the processes of the id, that is to say the impulses, needs, affects.

One can say that morality is stored in aims, as well as social norms, etc. Conscience is a feeling that is triggered by judgments of good or evil that are also generated by aims. "

"Pangs of conscience therefore arises when one has not behaved according to the moral ideas that have formed in one," concluded CP.

I nodded. "And if, for example, you committed an act that you believe you are guilty of."

"Why were such theories born?" asked CP. "They really don't depict the complicated processes in the brain."

"At that time, one did not know otherwise, theories of the time, which, like these, fell on fertile ground, because here the role of the unconscious was presented more clearly for the first time.

Until then, one had more or less thought that one dominates himself only with his consciousness. This theory was something new, the time was right and it was very simple.

The time was also ripe, because at that time the prudery was driven to the extreme, which led to sexual neurosis. That was a strong focus of this theory building.

Such theories can last a long time - like habits. And have been defended for a long time.

Freud pointed out that people are not always masters of their own houses - because unconscious currents can take control.

But with his division of the psyche into three separate areas, he unfortunately did not hit the facts.

Because the psyche arises from aims that form neural networks (midpoints) in order to reach it. Countless of these evolve in order to be able to survive and adapt in the world.

All are more or less connected with each other and act particularly depending on the current aims.

And one more word about the dreams:

What one dreams is not the essential; but how you yourself interpret your dreams.

Because then, through the research in your deeper SELF, aims are touched that otherwise can only, unconsciously, play along in the great concert of the psyche. Because, as a rule, they cannot be perceived by the midpoints during wakefulness for a wide variety of reason

For example:

In contrast to being awake, where adaptation aims with the cerebrum dominate, dreams are about issues of the respective living being that are no longer influenced by the midpoints. The cerebrum plays no role in this regard. This is how the fantasies of dreams are perceived as reality.

Sleep is about recovery from wakefulness, in which one can constantly be brought back from the midpoint into structures.

The dream is about the continued functioning of the senses, which are now directed inwards. Since many functions of the brain are changed, they show topics and processes that are not aimed at an end result - like the aims (although here too only substances run according to aims).

You shouldn't take your dreams so seriously. They are surreal stimuli, scenes or stories that arise through associations, similarities, etc. Overall,

however, they have little to do with
reality.

Psyche

Since people are shaped by aims, it is clear what it consists of.

▶How did it come about?

When life developed from matter, it wanted to continue to exist.

▶ What is its task?

It strives to carry out the aims inherent in each living being. The psyche serves to preserve life by adapting to the environment, including through feeling, thinking, learning.

▶ How does it work?

Through aims that have created neural network connections.

▶ Where is the psyche?

In the brain.

(Wikipedia definition: The brain is an organ of the central nervous system of all vertebrates and some invertebrates, which consists primarily of nerve tissue.)

The central point of all life is the command anchored in the psyche to follow one's feelings - especially the life instinct. It was formed around 3.5 billion years ago and continues to have an effect today.

> **The psyche therefore consists of the aims that are in the human brain, or that are formed and that move the person with the resulting centers, unconsciously or consciously.**

With regard to activity, which depends on the state and course of the external world and the state of the internal states, there are centers that act in the foreground or background and those that are currently passive (e.g. centers are ostensibly active in a new environment, social behaviors take place in the background in parallel, and passive are aims that are satisfied or not needed at the moment).

The midpoints are initially generated by aims and represent them.

This means that if a neural network is stimulated, the goal is activated.

Depending on the demands of life, new aims are constantly formed that generate centers.

(The processes of learning and un-learning take place in the synapses of the neurons).

Midpoints can become stronger or weaker in value - depending on when and how often they are needed. If they are no longer needed, they weaken and usually die out.

Psychological phenomena or func-tions, i.e. acts, states, patterns, experiences, are generally the ef-fects of neural networks that work together with other midpoints and generate feelings in parallel.

The midpoints are networked with each other depending on the aims, can form clusters (a grouping for certain processes) and usually always learn something new.

This means that the psyche in the brain remains flexible and adaptable.

The psyche is not the same as the soul, because it believes in super naturalistic elements.

Of course, faith can also be a center in the psyche and thus influence other neural networks.

This particularly applies to religious, mystical themes, which can cause a self-fulfilling prophecy in the person concerned through the resulting perspective, which can change their psyche and subsequently their body.

Psychological satisfaction and balance are evident when the midpoints harmonize with each other.

More or less imbalance arises, for example, when aims with their centers negatively influence the function of others beyond a healthy level. Or cannot be achieved. This can occur due to expectations that are too high.

Here you could say: satisfaction is usually based on the level of expectations.

So, if you are dissatisfied, you should look for the aims - and possibly modify them (change them or replace them with another aim).

Sleep and dreams create different patterns in the psyche because brain functions then work differently.

What the MIND is

> It is based on the human psyche.
> Driven by new or existing aims, the mind can jump from one neural network to other neural networks at lightning speed in order to track down information on how to achieve them.

It is further activated by these and searches for suitable facts in all neural networks accessible to him, which are temporarily stored in the new network that may have arisen through the respective aim in order to carry it out.

Mental flexibility therefore means searching and bun-

dling information and experiences on certain topics within milliseconds in these extensive organic neural networks, which cannot be compared with a computer.
Mental flexibility generates understanding, promotes creativity and is important for learning.

As a result, the neural networks (midpoints) can adapt to life and constantly create new ones.

Because the more immobile the mind and brain, the more one reacts like an automaton: new things are put into old drawers; and one keeps running after their information without incorporating the new.
But this would be important in order to create new solutions to a problem or to be able to deal with the world and oneself

better, more appropriately and to gain further insights.

So, the more rigid the brain, the less one thinks and re-acts - limited by a midpoint - often inappropriately and spontaneously.

So the human mind, driven by unconscious or conscious goals, seeks information in order to carry it out (consciously, if one pays attention to it).

It can appear suddenly, reappear elsewhere, etc.

The legal processes of the mind as information seekers depend on the aims to be carried out.

A good example of mental activity is thinking:

This always means concentrating on a topic, an aim, and what comes to mind in response to the questions posed by the brain – its huge organic networks.

This is caused by an internal or external impulse (from the sensors) that stimulates midpoints in the brain, which in turn activate the attention or consciousness to deal with the appropriate topic (questions, decisions, judgments, etc.). deal with, i.e. to obtain further (inner) information with the mind.

This process of thinking: impulse > midpoints > consciousness > mind > midpoints go on until you have a coherent feeling, you can't get any further or it is replaced by another topic.

Flexibility also means that you don't always accept quick reviews like this, but rather take a closer look at them if they are important to you.

In other words, you should look twice more so that consciousness (better: the sensors) is activated and sends information to the brain, with the aim that synapses (which are responsible for learning) can possibly change.

So, if you create an aim that takes into account the above, you can become more flexible, i.e., include other mid-points, experiences, similarities.

General definition:

> "Ghosts" can generally be called aims. Such as zeitgeist (goals that were current at a time) or the humanities, all of which have the goal of finding out something about their category that cannot be scientifically defined precisely - for example due to the complexity.

> What was one asked (by philosophers):
>
> ▶ How does the mind get into the machine (here: the human body)?
>
> Reply:
>
> ▶ It does not come into the "machine", but belongs to the brain from the moment it is created and is adequately expanded for its development.

Mind and brain are mutually depend-
ent in humans. There is no one without
the other!

Anyone who claims this anyway (such
as Descartes) drives a wedge into the
natural interrelationship and opens the
floodgates to misinterpretations regarding the psyche.

**Minds are structures that are
formed by aims.**

The more consciousness (with
his senses) is activated, the
better you can recognize the
world and yourself and give the
brain the opportunity to learn -
to form new aims or midpoints.

The faster midpoints can
change, i.e., the better they
learn and interact with other
midpoints, the more adaptable
and flexible the brain is in
reaching aims.

The flexibility of the mind depends on the disposition, what
has been learned in the course

of life and the current condition of the person.

> **One more remark about the "mind"**: A mind, in the sense of an immaterial being, which our ancestors felt internally and then projected outwards, because the functioning of the brain - also with regard to the central mechanism - was completely unknown to them, only exists in humans. Everything else is projections that have no substance in reality.

THE SELF

> **The SELF is a relatively small, but - in terms of its values - an essential part in the human brain - and also acts from this.**
>
> **Among other things, it decides through control efforts with - over its respective midpoints, which have formed from its aims.**

It is initially formed from feelings: what I like, what I don't like. Over time, this changes to: I want that, I don't want that. And the SELF forms itself accordingly. The aims are correspondingly stored in the brain and work unconsciously or consciously.

Depending on the level of development, they are supplemented with cognitive personal aims.

That SELF can control areas of the psyche up to certain limit thresholds and, if necessary, influence them more or less with his will. So overcome other goals in his psyche via the midpoint mechanics.
But the stronger the feelings, the more difficult it becomes.
In general: The more the feelings have power in the goals, the more difficult it is for the mind.
This has to be explained - not feelings! These run according to the laws inherent in them, which can make it difficult for the mind to influence.

This will also have to do with the fact that people have developed through feelings in the course of their evolution - the mind only much later.

Also for this reason - and because it is much easier than using the mind - feeling is often preferred.

The SELF, that is, what you mean, what you are yourself, as I said, is formed from the feelings of human being, from his mental state. The beginning is around the end of the 2nd year of life.

Here personal aims gradually emerge.

One more word about SELF-Ideal:

This is how you would like to be yourself and how you mean how others should see you.

This can harm you if you set aims incorrectly.

Free will

Example: The brain (in which the SELF with its aims is also located) makes a decision that can become conscious a millisecond later.

This then evaluates the feeling in such a way that the consciousness has decided.

This is also because the processes in the brain are difficult to follow.

Since one has the feeling of having made free decisions with one's consciousness and will, people believe in free will.

And then, as a rule, don't question this.

If you were to do this again experimentally, you would have clear evidence that the aims in the brain always decide.

Because the respective will is also an aim (among other aims).

Where did these aims come from? - In the brain.

Absolute freedom would mean being completely independent, including from the brain. But logically this cannot be the case.

One can only say "free" in relation to "free from". One can never be free from everything. In particular, the will cannot be free from all the aims of the brain.

A free will, which means that one is independent of everything, is therefore an illusion.

So one would inevitably come to the conclusion that consciousness has never decided anything with its so-called "free will". Because consciousness is only there to perceive with the senses and to transmit this information to the brain.

The conclusion would be that there is no such thing as free will.
On the other hand, the feeling that this "freedom" would otherwise have to be given up will usually defend itself. And for this it "works" with the midpoint-mechanics.

This can create an aim that is no longer aware of opposing arguments.

So, the feeling of freedom becomes an aim that evokes positive sensations; one can then feel free from all constraints by hiding evidence to the contrary.

Such as:

In connection with the refutation of free will, it is often argued that one would then no longer have any responsibility, since everything had already been determined and one could excuse everything.

Apart from the fact that this is not a scientific argument, I recommend reading my article on guilt. It is clearly stated here that man is guilty if he has broken the laws agreed upon by the community in which he lives.

Aims run according to the midpoint mechanics. These devalue everything that does not fit the respective aim. Such as the above consideration, which leads to the recognition of the lack of freedom of the will - if one does not accept that.

Now one can argue: of course, free will accesses the brain, but it is above it because it decides for itself what it accesses.

I would strongly recommend anyone who argues like this to take a close look at how the brain works. In order to see how diverse it is and how it is tailored to the respective aims, it constantly adapts to the respective information it receives from its senses.

Originally to ensure survival and then to achieve the respective aims.

Conclusion: Certainly, the will, as the aim, can decide. But each time it did not arise out of nothing, but out of the brain with its many aims. And ultimately, depending on strength, this more or less decides on the aim of the will!

It is also not free, because a number of factors, some of which are unknown, always co-decide, over which one often has no influence.

The will that resides in the brain is a sustainable aim, with a very strong Midpoint. In other words, a dynamic neural network that has a greater influence on other networks.

A strong will is important so that one does not succumb to wrong aims.

This will of the SELF with its midpoints can more or less bring the brain into

corresponding structures via their mechanics.

If you were stronger than other aims
that opposed the will aim, then one
speaks of self-overcoming .

Free will should therefore mean that it
is not subject to legal processes - like
everything else. Anyone who walks
through the world with open eyes will
have to admit that this is just a wish
that the facts (substances) do not cor-
respond to.

Because of course every will, which is
always an aim, runs according to laws.
In order to achieve it, one has to find a
suitable path.

And, as I said, the substances on this
path also run according to certain
laws.

Hence the word "free" is downright
wrong.

The central im-portance of aims

(Conversation about)

With the topic:

Gestalt Psychology

Universal scholar

Consciousness Restriction

Thinking habits

Life Attitudes

Fear of death

Thirst for knowledge

If you want to know yourself, ask about your aims.

**The most essential point is
their nature: If they are not
fulfilled, they urge, depending on the instantaneous or
general value in oneself with
feelings, to be somehow
achieved after all.**

**"Aims (often synonymous with
values) consist of networks of
neurons and synapses, among
other things. These act as knitting patterns and mark or generate a way to get there when
activated. In this way they
structure the brain and, in di-
rect succession, people and the
world. "**

"You say that all living beings are
aligned with aims. How did you
come up to this? "*CP* was curious.

"I was wondering why people do what they do. And have repeatedly observed that aims (as midpoints) shape people - as long as they are in the waking state of attention. "

"And outside of wakefulness?"

"Are they in sleep, or similar states in which the midpoints have slackened and the brain structure changes drastically.

The difference between to be awake and sleep is that in the former the midpoints provide structure; The frontal lobe has a significant share in the aims sought here. Whereas they are partially reduced to zero during sleep (the forehead brain is then partially blocked - such as the logical functions). So, the midpoints have little influence on the brain, which can therefore conjure up the strangest images.

Not infrequently it is somehow stimulated emotions that are experienced unbridled as reality with vivid fantasies.

So, other mechanisms and laws are active.

But of course, everything continues according to substances and laws - only according to other aims."

"How do you define aims?"

"Form a structure that leads to the desired endpoint of a path. For this, two things are needed: First, man must form a structure in himself and he must see the world in a structure that shows a suitable path. And that's how all living things do it, because their original goal is survival. "

"That means that the living being structures itself, takes itself into a different shape?" Asked CP.

"No, the respective aim is this form".

"Aims are very important in your theory building," stated CP.

"In fact, everything is structured," I nodded. "Take the system life. In every living being, there is a spectrum of aims that relativize, detach, connect with each other, form co-operative groups, cover up, wrestle for supremacy, and organize themselves into a partially alternate hierarchy. Aims are added, others change or go out. Each target has, or generates, its opponent, if other targets are touched and run the risk of being compromised. And every action takes place through a set of aims that each develop structures, compromise, reinforce or weaken. Many aims change in the course of life, except for the very low-lying, for example, the life instinct. This one always remains, even if you are very old."

"That sounds very complicated," said CP.

"It is, too," I nodded again. "The whole system is incredibly diverse and nested. That makes it so difficult to tell exactly where the driving forces of action come from.

Every behaviour, if traced back, will have its source in the life instinct. There are usually many intermediate stages between this and the current behaviour. That's why it's often hard to find the connections. But the younger a living being, the easier it is to determine. In the course of his life man differentiates more and more. It builds up more and more, depending on the aims it carries. "

"Can you never get to the bottom of the psyche?"

"Not in the slightest. Because you constantly adapt to internal and external changes. But if you want to try to recognize yourself, it helps to know that everything is designed in one of midpoints - like the aims of the SELF, which are in the brain and play an important role.

Ultimately, people are always circling around the same aims, only the content is different. The ultimate aim is, as a rule, the life instinct, which, it seems, always wants to grow, wants more and higher, closely followed by the aim of orientation, showing man his environment, which is of value to him, in positive or negative Meaning, in order to be able to react accordingly. The most important design factor is then the group - starting with two people - the society in which one lives. The aim of being recognized is arguably one of the strongest in life. Thus, the society in which one lives can totally become one's own world, that is, it can express one's aims, in other words: Values that have been anchored in the socialization process can absolutely shape you and cannot lead to other aims in this regard."

"You say there's no life without a midpoint?"

"Let me redefine what I mean by 'midpoint': it means the world that is created to reach an aim. Everything else
is more or less shielded. He selects
from what he finds and believes he has
a value for the aim, and gives shape to
the world. Imagine the unimaginable:
completely without aims. In you, the
aim would no longer be to survive, to
satisfy your needs, to orient oneself.
From the very beginning of the first life
in the world, you would find the aim of
survival, which created the 'sight' and
brought the found world into a form.

A strong aim can completely take over
the human being for a period of time
and structure it completely. This can
be seen very well in the phenomenon
of love, or when you have a task in
front of you that completely engages
you. Everything in one is aligned as
much as possible."

"You meant the aims in man are hier-
archical. Are you saying that there is a
command center in the brain?"

"No, this is not existing. What I mean
by this is that the more important the

aims are, the higher the rank. To achieve this, neural networks join together to form jointly acting groups, ensembles. The hierarchy can change constantly according to the demands of the world."

"When and how did these networks actually come about?"

"Human brain development begins in the third week of pregnancy and is largely complete only 20 to 30 years after birth.

The baby already has almost the entire amount of neurons at the time of birth, but only a small part of the neuron processes and synapses. These multiply after birth at a breathtaking pace and network the neurons, it forms a lot of networks.

These are then reinforced or dissolve again. "

"According to what rules?"

"According to the respective aims. It depends on what value they have in relation to the aims in the brain and how intensively they are used. The experiences with the environment determine which nerve networks become stronger, endure and which do not. "

"So, the decisive factor for this are the experiences that the living being has in the various phases?"

"The more important something is for a living being, the more it learns in this relationship. Neuronal networks are amplified, reshaped or re-formed."

"Do the individual neurons only react to a specific impulse?"

"No, they can form structures for different impulses with different neurons, they have a multiple function, so to speak: For the respective aims, many nerve cells have the possibility, in milliseconds, of an impulse with other cells, which have an equal potential in themselves to organize.

Take about a life-threatening situation. This structure over various activated neurons lightnings fast your shape.

The more life, the survival is affected, the stronger the activities. "

"So, no order is given from 'above'?"

"The 'command' is the perception, the impulse, which is then translated into reactions - if there is an aim for it, and the impulse has the corresponding valence."

"What determines the valence?"

"The aims that lie in one."

"But if you say that the life instinct is usually at the top of the hierarchy, then it would have to be found some- where!"

"It lies in the primordial structures of living beings that have passed it on through DNA."

"If one could define the aims in hu- mans as associations of neurons, which u. a. are stimulated by stimuli to form a figure? "

"Yes. And in the same way that neurons can have multiple functions, so too are the individual aims: they can organize themselves into groups - into aims that can form action forms. At the same time, various aims are being stimulated in parallel, forming together forms. "

"Let me repeat: the impulse, the stimulus from outside or inside activates targets, these activate further neural networks and these again solution programs."

"That's the procedure," I confirmed.

"When you go from one midpoint to the other, is it like switching from one neural network to another?"

"Yes, the midpoint is made up of co-operating networks with their respective weights."

"Once again asked: Everything is subject to aims?"

"Yes, whether inorganic or organic."

"So not just the living beings?"

"Look: After the big bang there was mostly hydrogen, helium and some lithium and beryllium. From these gases galaxies with solar systems and planets developed under great pressures, and all the elements we know today formed during this time. All this was inorganic until a certain point in time. "

"And was shaped based on aims?"

"When substances or their environment are changed, different forms and laws result.

Everything has the aim of forming a figure according to the laws. Exactly that is also subject to everything organic. What they all have in common is that they are guided by aims. From this perspective, there is no difference between the inanimate and the animated. With the latter, 'only' the aims of survival are added, which have led to ever more complex structures.'

"Why do you often not see that aims shape you?"

"Quite simply because you believe you are shaping yourself with your consciousness."

--- Gestalt psychology ---

After a break, *CP* continued.

"You certainly know **Max Wertheimer**, who said: 'There are relationships in which not everything that happens as a whole derives from the way the individual pieces are and are composed, but conversely, where - in a pertinent case - what, what in a part of this whole happens, determined by internal structural laws of this its whole. '"

I nodded. "These internal structural laws result from aims in man; they record for what he is receptive to, important to him, and save this as a wholeness. For example, listening to music is, of course, the melody and not the individual instruments. This holistic view is an important feature of all living things. "

"Wertheimer's Gestalt theory, then, seeks to clarify the laws by which the brain joins elements into a whole," concluded *CP*.

"These are explained neither by the laws of the individual parts nor by their sum," I added. "But they are explained by the respective aim in the human being, which brings all parts with its midpoint into a structure appropriate to the aim, which is then stored in the brain.

Holistic recognition makes sense to handle situations better and faster. "

"I'll summarize it again," said *CP*. "The holistic view of the brain has the aim of being able to make quick decisions - if it were to go into all the details every time, then this delays its capture or its decision. This holistic view arises in man through experiences that he has already made in similar situations. But since these are only similar, that does not necessarily mean that they are

appropriate for an aim or that it correctly indicates a lying one. "

"Right. As a rule, this results in a figure that can be dealt with without losing himself in details.

--- Universal scholar ---

"And you say everything in the universe is shaped by aims," *CP* was curious.

"Everything has the aim to form a figure according to the respective laws.
Everything is aligned with aims. "

"Even a lifeless stone?" CP smiled.

"By 'lifeless stone' you probably mean
something lying around somewhere.
Well, I would like to say: First, there is
movement within the stone, because it
consists of atoms or even smaller par-
ticle waves, which are not motionless
and also run according to laws. And
secondly, when this stone is moved,
then it forms with its environment, the
circumstances of a particular structure
according to the laws. That's what I

mean when I say: everything has the aim of forming a figure according to the laws."

"Could a stone form a structure even without laws?"

"How come? This is impossible because the laws are inherent in the substances. Nothing can happen without laws, because the substances are laws! "

"And so, you came to the conclusion that everything has the aim of forming a figure according to the laws."

"Right, this happens completely automatically. It is not that a stone has a consciousness that is out to obtain information. He's not alive. But since, as I said, everything runs according to laws, the aim automatically arises to create structures according to the laws of nature.

The same thing happens to the living beings, except that here the aim of survival is added. This aim shapes the

human being. This is what I call midpoint or midpoint-mechanics.

Imagine a person who has no more
aims. So do not eat anymore, drink,
etc. What would happen to that? "

"He would probably die."

"By the way: without an aim, the pla-
cebo effect wouldn't work either. The
aim here is to achieve something
through medication. This creates a
midpoint that pulls in everything that
is useful for that aim. Of course, also
experiences that were made when you
were already taking any medication
that helped. The logic of the brain is:
If a suitable drug, which comes from a
competent person, is taken against
this disease, then this aim will also be
fulfilled.

As a result, the previous internal structure in this relationship can change up
to the fulfillment of the aim: from ill-
ness to health."

"And this is done by the brain just because it "recognized" a drug that helps in his view?"

"Yes, that is enough. Unless, for example, the consciousness (better: the perception of the senses) gives the information that there is no active ingredient in the drug or that one does not trust the person who prescribed it. This would severely limit or negate the effect.

--- Consciousness restriction ---

The vast majority of human reactions are unaware. Consciousness becomes only a very small part, and always when something important occurs. Then information about the consciousness is obtained. If they are relevant, the brain processes them with the midpoints.

All other reactions and behaviours take place via the general, more or less strong, attention or automatically. "

(Senses attention; takes in the outside and inside world with the senses loose-

ly - consciousness, i.e. increased attention, is specifically concerned with
something.)

(Attention of the senses; takes in the
outside and inside world with the
senses loosely - consciousness of the
senses, i.e. increased attention, is
specifically concerned with something.)

"But that must be an incredible
amount of aims with their midpoints
that shape the people!"

"Yes, you can say that. Just such a
simple act as picking up a newspaper
requires many learned aims that have
been summarized and then run automatically.

Time and again, I hear that people
have trouble understanding that everything is guided by aims, including
themselves. I think its daily life that
makes them fail to understand that
sentence. Because everything is so
natural, what happens. If they dig
deeper, then they could see that every
action, every movement is guided by

aims and moves them. For example, the handle to the glass of water and drink from it. "

"Many people I've talked to actually have trouble understanding what 'aim' means," *CP* nodded. "For them, one aim is to complete a task or strive for something. But such a simple thing, such as bringing a spoon to your mouth, is not an aim for them!"

"Because it runs automatically, without paying more attention to this process. If they were to get to the bottom of this, they would come closer to the fact that every single hand movement must first be learned. The motivation for this was aims.

Because that's just the treachery for the realization that simple actions are taken for granted and not further think about it. Not realized that very specific aim-oriented processes are behind it."

"Yes, that's right," CP remarked thoughtfully.

"Lots of amazing achievements by people who are often based on island talents, for example to remember a large number of things in a limited time, to perform complex arithmetic operations in a few seconds or to learn a new language in a short time, would not be possible without an aim. This provides the structure that leads to the solution. Even artificial intelligence, which works with algorithms, does not come to a conclusion without a specified aim. "

--- thinking habits ---

I took a short break.

Then I continued: "Until the 16th century, people knew virtually no laws. Everything was determined from God's perspective. But even in our time, many are far from seeing everything controlled by aims, thinking that most things happen by themselves anyway, and still viewing consciousness as something metaphysical or something. These views have passed from generation to generation and still shape some philosophers and people who deal with these issues. Everyone else usually just takes it that way because they do not even think about it. "

"Why don't man often see that aims shape him?"

"Simply because man believe that he shapes himself with his consciousness."

"What if they were to throw their antiquated views overboard and start thinking that consciousness is indeed just a brain information provider?"

"Most people are too caught up in their views, their habits of thinking. In the least, the aim is to get to the bottom of the processes in them, to deal intensively with the course of their consciousness, as with this topic. Added to this there are innumerable people who live in the world of esoteric mysticism and, if they accept this insight, injure their world. For them consciousness is an essential element in the mystical view of the world,

which is shaped by a metaphysical aim with its midpoint in them. "

"You mean they create this aim themself? "

"Secure. Without noticing it."

"The truth does not interest them, do you mean to say that," said *CP*.

"They are interested in the truth," I replied, "but only their truth". Everything else is labelled as nonsense.

One can call this the drama of the blinded human being. Its midpoint, the mystical world, surrounds it like a bell shielding all other views and evidence."

"Pity," regretted *CP*, "I find it always very exciting to hear and discuss new views."

"I feel the same way", I nodded. "Unfortunately, it is often the case that each of us has a world view that involves a more or less strong perseverance. Changes to beloved settings are reluctant to make.

For example, branded images and ideas of the culture in which you grew up are transported from generation to generation. Only too rarely are these questioned, and if so, often with bad feelings, because they question the structures they have created: in themselves and in society. Resistance quickly builds up, trying by all means to maintain the old structures. "

"Self-knowledge apparently does not belong to the aims of many people," said *CP*.

"I have that impression too. Self-knowledge comes through self-observation. Who does that?"

"Funny, I enjoy watching myself and sometimes have to laugh heartily when I've seen things wrong or insisted on an erroneous point of view. By introspection, one comes closer, sees moves in ones that have not yet noticed, especially in new or critical situations.

Maybe it's also because I can accept myself and my behaviour, with the sentence, 'What happened, had to happen as it happened.' "

"I feel the same way," I confirmed. "That's why I enjoy talking to you. I've learned a lot from you already. "

"The compliment I can give back, the discussions with you are very stimulating for me.

What aims should one have?", he continued.

"I can't answer that like that. The aim is to dictate something to others, not within me. Everyone has their own values. I can only speak for myself here, for my aims: The most important thing for me is knowledge. I can completely immerse myself in it.

What comes to mind is that dissatisfaction always depends on the level of expectation."

"You mean, the decisive factor is the respective goal?"

"The more you have achieved an aim, the higher the satisfaction - and vice versa. Here you can find roots for euphoria and especially depression.

Therefore, one should think carefully, which aims one undertakes. Are its wrong aims, for example, that cannot be achieved, then you open the door to bad mood or depression. False aims can severely burden the psyche. "

"Do you have ideals?"

--- life attitudes ---

"Not really, unless you count the truth."

"Would wealth and fame give you something?"

"If I had the sense of wealth, then I would have to write for the people according to their expectations. So, fairy tales, sex, crime. These would not be desirable aims for me. I am absolutely

139

satisfied with my life, in which I search for new insights. I have nothing of wealth, because what I want to know is primarily in me and rises spontaneously. So, much money would not help me in this respect.

And fame could possibly create vanity in me that does not help my actual aims, but rather hinders them. It could stop me from time to time questioning my theses and possibly insisting on them, even against legitimate objections.

There are enough examples of famous personalities. "

"You are different than most people."

"I did not aspire to that. I am the way I am, and that's how I take myself. "

"Why do people strive for greatness, for wanting to have more and more?"

"One reason will be vanity. An essential element of life is the recognition in the group, the society. The general reasons will lie in the primordial structures. "

"Therefore, people are striving for wealth, build taller buildings, clothe themselves conspicuously, show what they have, try to achieve a high position in society?"

"I think that's the driving force. Many people are shaped by this. "

--- fear of death ---

"Are you afraid of death?"

"I know that the midpoint of life-drive creates this fear to drive people to continue living. For example, it does not matter to him whether human being is terminally ill and suffers from horrible pain or only wishes to die. Knowing the reason makes it easier for me to deal with these feelings. And: If you're dead, the reason is gone anyway, then feelings logically play no role anymore."

"Why do many people think that death is something very bad?"

"Because the life instinct is fooling everyone. He is the strongest midpoint of life. "

"But he is ultimately only an aim."

"Naturally. Therefore, for example, the suicide is also nothing wrong. Anyone who believes this merely reflects his own opinion or that of the society in which he grew up or lives. "

"And the own opinion is always relative," *CP* added.

"What do you think about near-death experiences?" He asked.

"Dying is the extinction of the organ functions of a living being, which leads to death. Death is the function setting of the neural networks in the brain.

Experiences can always only be gained through the brain. And as long as this is not dead, it is capable of producing fantasies. When the brain is dead, you do not experience anything anymore.

Near-death experiences come clearly from the brain. And the brain is not always right with what's coming out of it - that we see very clearly in the dreams."

So, one should not attach great importance to near-death experiences."

--- thirst for knowledge ---

"Can one say, Mr. Hermsch, you are always on the trail of yourself?"

"That's not quite true, but I often spontaneously have thoughts and feelings that I follow, with which I study intensively. I research, compare, falsify and verify and try, if they help me in my desire to understand, finally to bring them understandable on paper. Hoping to get criticized if I'm wrong about a view.

In addition, there is a strange striving for perfection in the relationship that I want to answer questions that are in me to the smallest detail. These aims are sustainable in me, so even if I have answered questions, they pop up again and again and make me check to see if my answer was correct or had any errors. "

"From uncertainty?"

"Out of openness and the pursuit of perfection."

"So, it's not just the urge for an answer that makes you think of something, it's the urge for it?"

"Through this quest for perfection fall to me answers. And since these aims are sustainable in me, there seems to be no end to it. That's why criticism is important to me. And that's why I write.

In addition, dealing with a question always raises new questions. So, my urge to learn never actually comes to a conclusion.

Even while falling asleep and sleeping, there are suddenly thoughts or ideas, for example, about topics that I had once occupied myself with, but where I had no solution.

I then take notes for a moment, because I had the experience that if I did not write it down right away, the thoughts would have disappeared the next day. A voluntary retrieval of these target solutions is not possible for me after I wake up again. "

"All this seems to give you a lot," presumed *CP*.

"I can be completely absorbed in it", I confirmed.

How to perceive the world
(Definition and explanation)

One can look at the world as a fixed entity that is the same from every point of view.
This is called outside-in theory.

However, one can also see the world in such a way that different creatures see it differently in terms of their aims.
This is what I call the

inside-out theory.

There, as here, the sensors
receive stimuli from the
outside world. A few impulses are enough to get an
idea.

In contrast to the outside-
in theory, however, the
world is created by the respective living beings according to their goals:
The sensors send the recorded information to the neural
networks. If it is deter-
mined there that the world
they perceive differs from
that stored in the mid-
points, they may process
their view of the world.

This process can be followed immediately:

The world that living be-
ings, including humans, perceive is one that results
from **their aims that neural
networks have built up.**
(Just as after conception
the body builds itself according to inherited aims,
so does the psyche: **these
aims create neural networks**
in order to be reached.)

According to these, the sensors see the world. As soon
as the inner world differs
from the outer world, the

neural networks may change
their structures.

This is how man perceives
the world according to his
psychic aims.

!! The world that shows itself to us is of course there first, but what people absorb from it is decided by the brain according to its aims. !!

Even if you want to record everything that is around you, it always remains a matter of the limits of our senses and brain.

Wikipedia (definition): In living beings, perception is the process and the subjective result of information acquisition (reception) and processing of stimuli from the environment and from the body. This happens through unconscious (and sometimes conscious in humans) filtering and merging of par-

tial information into subjectively meaningful overall impressions. These are also called precepts and are continuously compared with stored ideas (constructs and schemes).

▶ According to this definition, there would be the world first, which is created by filtering and merging partial information into subjectively meaningful overall impressions in living beings.

This raises the question: According to which directives are the filtering and merging of partial information carried out?

The answer could only be: Through the aims in the brain, which are focused by means of the sensors, which are focused by its values (aims) (i.e. where the attention should be directed).

▶ **So, I think it's the other way around: that first the brain (the midpoints)**

has an approximate ex-
pectation about the world
according to its aims.
Then this is perceived by
the senses selected in
this way. Once this is
done, inequalities in
these two worlds (expec-
tation and fact) are cor-
rected by the brain in milliseconds when it feels
right according to its
aims.**

First of all, you always see the world according to your habits, expectations, and ideas that are stored in your brain about aims. If it recognizes (because it is valuable) that it deviates from it, then the perception is adjusted accordingly. Aims learn or form a new – again initially according to the aims that one has inherited or learned, because only through them can one originally perceive the world.

There is no world as it actually and always is, but only one

**from the perspective of the re-
spective observer.**

Therefore, we do not see the world as it appears to be in front of us (that is, the same for everyone), but one that the brain shows us based on its aims.

Since every person has their own characteristic aims, they also see their own world, to which they react individually.

(By the way, since each species has its specific goals, the world sees them similarly).

**Again: People can only perceive
the world from the perspective of
the respective observer.**

For clarification:

The world that we see is of course still there, even if we are no longer there. However, it would change according to the respective perception by other beings who are different from us.

Because there is no such thing as a world that is always the same.

What stays forever - no matter what perspective you look at it from - is that <u>identical substances under identical conditions always show identical results.</u>

Summarized:

> Human beings see the world from their point of view. This results from the aims of the respective person. Namely from his currently active ones or especially from those currently additionally stimulated.

▶ The active aims shape the world into a structure that is needed to achieve them.

▶ Depending on the value of the stimuli that are now activated, further aims are awakened, which additionally structure the view.

▶ So, there is ultimately no identical world that everyone sees the same, but many different, from the point of view of the respective aims.

And: intellect means to perceive something precisely, i.e. to understand it. You can only grasp what you have a system for.

(If one encounters something absolutely new, then of course one can also take in and grasp it - but, as I said, only according to one's predispositions aims). In this way, the new from the environment and inner field of the human being, from the brain, becomes his predispositions adjusted accordingly.

So, you absorb the world first through the aims in yourself and then with the aligned senses – in that order.

The senses are constantly confronted with unfiltered stimuli (approx. 11 million bits per second), but they do not simply represent the world in front of us 1:1, but the brain selects them with its aims, which align the senses in such a way that they only perceive the information that fits the aims of the brain because it is important.

These million bits are not there to depict the environment precisely for us, but to compare the structures that arise after selection through our aims with those stored in the brain and, if necessary, to correct them by learning (changing synapses).

In general, then, man has his hereditary world in the head brain, the autonomic nervous system (plus the somatic nervous system) and the abdominal brain (enteric nervous system), along with those who have experiences and learning were built in him.

This is the reason why we each perceive the world differently and possibly wrongly; because we weren't in the right midpoints. (Wrong in relation hung that we have disadvantages, e.g., not respond appropriately.)

And since the selection by the aims also influences the storage of experiences in the brain, this can lead to incorrect information.

A little excursion to objectivity:

How do animals, bacteria and viruses perceive the world?

And who sees the world more correctly?

Of course, people will say: the world ultimately looks the way we see it.

Anyone who says you can only see the world from a human perspective is definitely **right**.

Anyone who believes that this is being said about a basic world that is eternal and unchangeable is certainly **wrong**.

Because the world is basically **not** in an eternally identical state (because processes are constantly taking place on all levels).

A little incentive to think:

What should the brain also perceive when you say you see it for what it is?

The answer is only possible in relation to aims that reside in oneself - in the brain.

And: people's perception is limited. As for hearing and seeing with the respective bandwidth. Or e.g., the inability to perceive radioactivity, magnetism, ultrasound, etc.

There is no world that is the same and unchangeable from every perspective.

Summarized:

Viewed from living beings, the world is subjective.

Recorded by an apparatus - regardless of the perspective - it is always objective.

But this does not mean: forever fixed and immutable, because the world is constantly changing.

Only the laws according to which substances move are eternal.

And all perspectives of the macro- or micro world result in the sentences:

> **● Identical substances under identical circumstances always give identical results.**
> **● The reason for this is that everything is subject to unchangeable laws.**

158

● If you change substances or circumstances, then other laws also appear.

If you turn 180 degrees in a strange environment, it takes milliseconds before you consciously perceive what is in front of you.

This attaches to the brain: First, the general perception occurs according to its expectations. (If there are no specific ones, it looks for similarities). Depending on the extent to which this does not match what is in front of you, it is corrected if it is relevant.

The aim of orientation requires data from the senses to clarify whether and to what extent the world shown by the brain may deviate from reality in order to be able to adapt. This takes milliseconds. (The aim of orientation is a central aim in living beings).

Recognition also takes place through aims; one recognizes what was stored in the brain. This is also where the reason for confusion can be found (because the brain searches for similarities).

The selected stimuli may change existing neuronal networks in the brain or generate new ones if aims (midpoints) in the psyche consider this to be important. If the stimuli show more or less strong differences from what has been stored up to now, it is adjusted.

By means of the senses, which send information to the brain via attention, this is always up to date - if the aims of perception are not restricted too much by certain (rigid) midpoints.

Without new information from the senses, the brain is virtually blind - and only acts according to the previous information it had stored - as happens in a dream.

First you see the world that you last saved in yourself. If the senses recognize this differently, the storage changes - if the brain decides, this is important.

> E.g., when a landscape that has been seen fleetingly but assessed as irrelevant is seen by the senses. (The brain stays with its vision). <

> It is different when, for example, you wake up from sleep and the world saved before going to bed has changed. At first you see - expected - the world after the routine storage. But if the senses send other stimuli, then the brain will include them in its vision, because it is usually important in order to be able to deal with the immediate world.
The evaluation and any change take place very quickly (as I said: in milliseconds). <

> This is also how it happens in dreams: the senses, which are directed inward due to sleep, take the stimuli of the dream world as facts that the brain - and consequently we - take as

Regarding knowledge, individual things are not important. It all depends on the aim. If this is to look at details, only then will these be particularly perceived. But when it comes to saving the overall impression, then you perceive it as a whole.

The perception of music can serve as an example: You perceive the whole and not the individual instruments, because that is not the aim. (The whole thing is to perceive the feeling of music). The perception of individual devices would cloud the perception, because it could lead to other central points and be distracted.

This is exactly how you absorb everything in daily life from your goals. And that's how you see the world.

If something is no longer correct (e.g., something dangerous appears) then a target is activated in order to perceive it specifically. This suddenly puts you in a different focus. This is also recorded holistically and creates a different pattern in the brain.

Again: How and with what a room is filled is initially not important as long as one is aiming to perceive this room. Only when you look more closely through other aims do they gain value.

Conclusion: the brain always absorbs holistically. The stimulated aims can change the topics quickly.

How the brain works

(Definition and explanation)

> **The brain, which also contains the SELF with its aims, interprets all information and makes all decisions based on the aims it contains – which contain cognitive and intuitive parts.**

- The brain directs and moves people.

- It is not that the brain is there on the one hand and the SELF is on the other, but this is integrated in the brain and plays its role from here.

- And to prevent a widespread misunderstanding: consciousness is not the SELF!

164

The brain is an interpreter: it inter-
prets the world and events in a way
that suits its aims. It has the task of
interpreting perceptions and sensations (i.e. information) according to
the aims it contains and generating
appropriate attitudes and instructions
for action.

(It does not simply depict the world,
but shapes it - according to its aims.)
This is done by the midpoints (neural
networks).

This includes anticipating alternatives,
and et al to ask the consciousness of
what the particular problem solution
might have consequences (so that it
experiences it and gives information to
the brain) - unless it already "knows"
the consequences through similarities
that it has stored.

Again: The brain does not simply depict the world, but shapes it - according to its aims. This is done by the
neural networks (midpoints).

All decisions for the individual are
made by the brain in the head, the

autonomic nervous system (plus the somatic nervous system) and the abdominal brain (enteric nervous system).

Between these there is a constant exchange of information by means of neural networks.

Anyone who has ever been in a research facility in which the constant firing of neurons is made audible, gets an impression of the countless processes that take place in the brain.

The general knitting pattern of the brain is the similarity; When an impulse, a question, a request, etc. comes up, it first looks for something that equals it.

The brain is subject to physical and chemical laws. It runs, as I said, for similarities, themes and aims with their midpoints that control it, and consists of various areas. For example, Amygdala, hippocampus, hypothalamus, cerebellum.

Certainly e.g., mainly activated by the eyes the visual center (occipital lobe) in the brain, by hearing the hearing center (the auditory cortex) etc., but also always neural networks (mid-points) at the same time.

The first is physical, the second psychic.

It is important to know that these areas never work separately for themselves, but always with others via neural networks.

These in turn have connections to many other networks, so that ultimately the entire brain in the head, the autonomic nervous system (plus the somatic nervous system) and the abdominal brain (enteric nervous system) are interconnected.

All networks were created by aims. The neurons located here are not only bound to them, but can also be used for others via synapses.

Networks are particularly activated by essential information of the attention. The feelings have special value, which are always activated in parallel with the respective networks. They are particularly suitable for controlling people. This control takes place through the respective similarities in the brain, which only contain limited new information.

Like everything, the brain also runs after substances that are controlled by laws.

The aims of the SELF are also in the brain. The SELF consists of a relatively small set of aims, but they are – with respect to their values – an essential part of the brain. It can, with its will, and by means of the information of the perception, intensify or weaken aims, thus influencing other aims in the brain via the midpoint-mechanics of the will aim.

However, if you want something, then an aim can be generated – but whether this works, decides the psyche and the respectively activated midpoints in the brain with.

One does not experience oneself as someone controlled by the brain; because one does not perceive its processes, except for the decisions; because of the diversity cannot perceive. Therefore, one has the impression that one decides oneself, with his free will, his consciousness.

Not least because of this, the general view is that man controls himself with his consciousness and that the brain is only an aid

So, we do not experience our brain, but what our senses convey to us via the brain.

People see, feel the result of their thinking, their actions and think that they did this (for example with their free will or with their consciousness).

They are wrong! That's what her brain did.

Because if you look more closely, you learn that you are not something separate from your brain that looks at the brain from the outside, but that you are integrated into it.

When observing, the aim of observation, which has formed as a midpoint of the brain, is to observe the brain.

I would like to point out that consciousness in particular does not control man. This becomes clear when one looks at the awareness that it is just a brain information provider (so that it can better make its decisions).

It can only come to someone from his brain. Even if something comes to mind from the environment, it is always up to the brain to decide what value it may have to be taken into account.

Someone asked if one was a slave to his brain.

My Answer: The brain is not something alien, separate from the SELF - as the question sounded.

The SELF is in the brain with its aims and plays its role with many others, what I say already.

Without the brain, you are nothing. **With the brain**, one is everything that one feels, thinks, experiences, etc. daily. Here, too, are all the aims that the SELF wants to achieve.

And this will of the SELF, with its midpoints over its mechanics, with appropriate exercise and favourable psyche, can more or less bring the brain into appropriate structures.

One could only speak of slavery here if one has a weak will, or a strong (wilful) aim suppresses other (healthy) aims.

Everything that one perceives, recognizes, absorbs, thinks about, what comes to mind, etc., can form aims that reinforce others or generate new ones. Each new target creates or amplifies synapses, neural networks that work to achieve that aim. Once an aim has formed, it can play a role in the psyche.

The brain is constantly learning - by strengthening or rebuilding the synapses.

That's why it's so important to stay flexible in the brain (this is of course also an aim).

When a target is activated, such as when you want to grab a glass, then a trained cluster that consists of neural networks acts. This includes various areas in the brain to accomplish this task: estimating the distance to the glass, the size, weight, muscle and strength needed to lift it, etc. This is a brain work that we take for granted appears and usually occurs without conscious perception.

When you observe two people who talk animatedly: how they speak, their body language, the facial expression, the changing of their eyes, etc., then you have to wonder what the brain (and only this one) can do and does. This all comes from midpoints that are more or less co-ordinated with each

As a rule, automatic, learned behaviours are used.

It is often forgotten that people are only living beings who have developed from inorganic substances and, like these, are shaped by laws.

The main difference between humans and other living beings is their brains, which are capable of forming exorbitant neural networks with which they can recognize laws and create new processes.

And - with which an infinite number of fantasy structures can be imagined.

Midpoint-mechanics

(A key to the psyche)

(Definition and explanation)

> **The function of the midpoint mechanics is generated in the psyche due to an aim to be achieved.**
>
> **This means that anything else that doesn't fit or interfere with that aim will be depreciated as much as possible during this process.**

Midpoints are neural networks generated by aims, which then represent and execute them.

They are not rigid, but are constantly changing in terms of adapting to the environment and the inner world.

As already mentioned, other midpoints (neuron networks) that do not match are automatically reduced in value or switched off by the brain during this process.

As a rule, this is not perceived by humans.

He only recognizes what the midpoints in the brain show him.

Midpoints consist of neurons distributed far and wide across the brain, which involve many areas and form a network that serves to form attitudes, actions, ideas

and especially feelings

to create.

Depending on the flexibility of the respective brain, there are always new networks in addition to the existing ones, which are formed, among other things, by adapting to the outside or inside world (lightning-fast or gradually).

Many focal points are saved, changed or deleted for these reasons, among others.

While everything in the universe is shaped by aims who "don't care" about the consequences of their desired structure, with living beings the aim of preservation is added (to survive).

This takes place in the brain through networks of neurons and synapses, which I call "midpoints". Depending on the type and individual, the living beings are shaped by them.

As a general knitting pattern, the example of how to learn to ride a bike:

In the beginning there is
the aim. This creates a neural network in the brain to
reach it.

Balance, muscles, tendons,
posture, mental processes,
etc. are developed as sub-
goals in the required form,
coordinated with one another
and temporarily stored.

So gradually the skills are
improved; you learn from
your mistakes.

This is all done by the neural networks formed by the
aim of cycling and then further evolving to expand

> body-psyche coordination and fine-tune adjustments.
>
> The network at the beginning (the focus of cycling) has now become far-reaching interdependencies. Which, when the respective sub-goals have been achieved, are stored permanently and become an automatic behaviour that is activated when you get back on the bike.

Midpoints are thus created by aims and are their tools.

Neural networks connect areas of the brain such as: frontal lobe, cerebral cortex, cerebellum, limbic system, amygdala, language midpoint, visual cortex, hearing center, taste center, etc., and access memory content and everything that goes with it.

There is also a constant exchange of information with the autonomic nervous system (plus the somatic nervous system) and the enteric nervous system (which is also called the 'abdominal brain').

Midpoints act in such a way that they allow everything that could help to achieve or maintain their structure - the aim - and do not take everything else into account as far as possible.

This can then continue to work unconsciously.

Whoever becomes aware of this mechanism also understands a great deal about the functioning of his own psyche.

In general, the midpoints play the concert of life with one another; many processes take place at the same time.

In extreme cases, however, one midpoint can greatly reduce all the others so that only this midpoint shapes people, for example in phases of panic, ecstasy or when one is about to achieve maximum performance.

But even in the spectrum between normal and extreme, all midpoints act in such a way that they limit or strengthen others in value.

Making the midpoint-mechanics clear to other people is also so difficult because they are always in some aims without really noticing it properly. They don't look at their psychological processes.

What is even less perceived is that a lot no longer plays a role due to the respective aim.

One should perhaps have had the experience that one's view of the world can change in fractions of a second in order to understand it better.

I formed the term "midpoint-mechanics" in order not to always use neural-network-laws. He makes it clearer in a more memorable way that a neural network mechanically reduces or strengthens others in value, depending, as I said, whether they are unsuitable or suitable for the current midpoint.

And one more hint:

> **Most of the explanations about how the brain works boils down to the fact that certain areas are activated and react to stimuli.**

But never only one area reacts, rather a neural network (which connects different areas via synapses) is activated by the stimuli, which, if necessary, communicates with others.

> *You could compare it to preparing a meal:*

Knowledge plays an important role. In other words, what you need in what quantity, which procedure must be followed, what the hands or devices have to do, what amount of energy is required, whether the taste is right, etc. All of this works together in the right amount and forms that Meal.

Applied to the work of the brain to achieve an aim, this means that each brain area contributes a limited part that activates the responsible neural network in order to come to a successful conclusion.

<blockquote>Just as the ingredients etc. are not used without restriction, so is the brain. Here a neural network is in charge, there the recipe.</blockquote>

Perhaps the terms "selective attention" and "flow" help to improve understanding. With the first, only certain information that fits an aim is perceived from a lot of information. With the second one is in a state of flux that is only determined by one aim and does not allow anything else, i.e., is not disturbed by anything.

Both also apply to the midpoint point mechanics. Here, however, there is also the reference to the strict regularity with which perception is restricted. This means that the brain only perceives what is essential for the respective aim or aims. Everything else is absolutely not noticed and is virtually non-existent.

So, nothing is rated negatively or suppressed (accordingly, it does not trigger any reactions). So, the process is not disturbed by anything; one only lives in the world of the respective aim.

Without the midpoint point mechanics, the brain would plunge into chaos because aims could no longer be pursued permanently.

As I said, it is relatively seldom that people are shaped by only one midpoint. As a rule, many processes take place at the same time, all of which run according to the midpoint-mechanics and, depending on their value, are more or less important for other aims. This creates for example certain clusters that execute processes together.

In one sentence:

The more the brain pursues an aim, the less there will be other aims that do not contribute to it can, perceived or can work.

In this context, the experiment with a large number of people with a video of 75 seconds duration that the scientists Simons and Chabris carried out and called it "gorillas in our midst" is perhaps also interesting:

The film shows two teams with three players each, one wearing white and the other black T-shirts. The members of each team play a normal orange basketball by throwing or dribbling. After 44 to 48 seconds, something unexpected happens: a smaller person, completely wrapped in a gorilla costume, walks across the screen in the same way as the players. During these unexpected events, the basketball players unwaveringly continue their actions.

Before the test subjects see a video, they are given the task of either con-

centrating on the team in white or on the team in black and counting all rallies of the observed team in their heads or counting the thrown and dribbled rallies separately. After the test subjects have seen the video and completed their observation task, they are asked to write down their numbers. Then you ask them if (a) they noticed something unusual while counting, (b) if they noticed anything other than the six players, if someone else appeared in the video, finally: (c) Do you have a gorilla see going through the picture?

About half of the subjects did not notice the gorilla.

My comment on this: The given aims (the midpoints) did not allow everything else (including the gorilla) to be perceived.

On the basis of this experiment one can clearly see how a midpoint - here the task - works.

And one more note: wizards and hyp-
notists all work with the midpoint-
mechanics.

Finally:

> Who hasn't wondered why people
> can do something that goes far
> beyond "normal" behaviour - in a
> positive or negative sense.
>
> Here, too, the midpoint mechanics
> is the key to understanding them.

Because with it you can make all extreme behaviours clear.

> **Two examples for a better understanding:**

You are talking to someone about a topic (so you are in the midpoint of it). Suddenly you have the feeling that the other person is insulting you.

This can result in a new midpoint playing along, which weakens the previous one.

You are on your way to work and are thinking about the work ahead of them.

Suddenly you witness a robbery and your mind is at the midpoint of it.

If you look back at your situation later, you will see that you no longer had any of the thoughts before the attack. This new mid-point has reduced everything else to zero.

Appendix

Non-perception due to the midpoint - mechanism vs. repression

"If you say: 'A midpoint prevents you from perceiving something', then you get to the point much more accurately than if you say: 'You have repressed something'."

"I understood it like this," CP summed up: "An aim has to be achieved. To do this, a certain structure is needed. This is created from what is relevant to it, everything else is ignored. If something is disturbing, its value is reduced, so it has much less influence on the person."

I nodded. "This reduction of the other values does not happen intentionally, but mechanically. It is a lawful process. That is why I called it 'midpoint - mechanism'.

An example: On March 24, 2015, a pilot committed suicide in a passenger plane. He steered the plane into a rock massif. He took all 150 passengers with him to their deaths.

What was going on in this person's head?

The answer is provided by the midpoint - mechanism: the aim of taking one's own life reduced the value of all other midpoints (aims) or reduced them to zero; the impending collision with the mountains, the people who were on board and had to die with him, their relatives who had to suffer the loss, etc.

On the one hand, it is frightening what midpoints can do, including the terrible atrocities of the Nazi regime or inhumane acts that virtually all peoples committed."

"Or what individual people did to others," added CP.

"Yes. On the other hand, it is beautiful what midpoints can do. For example, love, standing up for people or other living beings.

"What can you do to escape a negative focus, not to be a slave to it and to expand your perception?"

"In quiet moments, look closely at it and ask yourself what aim is behind it.

Then: create a counter-aim and
link it to the midpoint. That
means: create a new aim that is
activated every time the impulse tries to provoke negative
behaviour, and thus dampens
and regulates it, influencing
your own behaviour more and
more.

Brain vs. Computer

The brain has the task of ensuring human survival; it is always active.

The computer has to perform arithmetic tasks that man has given up (with algorithms - a rule created in the language of the computer - which consists of a precise sequence of instructions with which certain tasks can be carried out in a given time to be done). To do this, it only has to be active until the work is done.

Calculation speed plays a secondary role for the brain; The connections of the neuron networks have priority.

The brain is a tissue that works according to organic laws - the computer is a calculator created from inorganic parts that needs specifications and cannot be creative by itself. Although it can calculate much faster than a brain, it lacks the creative element that enables creative solutions through endless linking possibilities:

Because the fact that the brain is busy with something, associations are very often stimulated: similarities. Often just any place you've been to and had a similar thought or feeling is enough:

If one wanted to build a computer that could be as creative as the human brain, this would probably be simply impossible: the computer would have to be infinitely flexible and be able to change its structure again and again at lightning speed. Not only information itself, but also all associations to it must be able to be linked. And this every time new information arrives.

That would be impossible for a machine whose basic substance is computing power. *Only biological substances like brains can do that.*

An essential control mechanism of human beings are feelings, which i.e., be generated by the brain.

It is not possible for a computer to generate feelings - similar to a human being.

The brain is there to form a structure according to the respective aims. These aims have been in the brain since time immemorial, or they are always new after they have been pro-created.

Everything in the brain can be influenced by everything. This must not be in the computer because otherwise he will not be able to carry out his bills - he will no longer be able to carry out his work step by step. He needs clear commands about what should be involved.

The central aim of the brain is that the living thing survives - adapts itself as possible to the environment. For this purpose, there are always various networks of neurons active in the brain that can constantly change their value flexibly.

The central aim of the computer is to calculate each time after the programming.

The brain carries out countless tasks at the same time and the priorities can change constantly - the computer is clearly overburdened here. It can only process a fraction of what the brain can do - and if so, then only with much more energy than the brain.

Many processes in the brain always run in parallel and new ones are constantly being added. There are always new synapses (which are responsible for learning) that strengthen or recede.

Processing steps in the computer can also be carried out in parallel. But nowhere near the size of the brain.

The computer needs clear relationships *- the brain draws conclusions from facts and (sometimes diffuse) information from outside and inside.*

This makes it possible for the brain to be creative. A computer cannot do that - for the reasons mentioned.

The brain is able to learn for a lifetime because it has to adapt to changing circumstances over and over again. This is not always the case, but is usually better for survival, because it can change flexibly again.

The brain is always active - the computer only when information arrives. *The brain never sleeps because it has to be careful about whether life is threatened – like a bird that is constantly on the lookout for danger.*

What can a person think of when naming the word red? Unprecedented associations, such as love experiences, traffic accidents, the setting sun, blood, colours of autumn, the cloth in the bullring, colour of flags, blast furnaces, etc.

What does the computer show when you enter red? A limited number of answers that humans have programmed once. There are only references (links) but no automatic associations (unless man links them). Feelings that are very strongly activated by the word red, for example, are lost on the computer because it is numb. *This is a huge benefit for humans because emotions are fine-tuning elements that are important to react and act.*

In this example - and no matter what word or concept it is - you can also see the difference between the brain and the computer very well.

The computer is a machine built by humans, the aim of which is to calculate. It does not use components that have nothing to do with each other - that do not fit into its strict logic-based calculation.

For example, a captcha - randomly arranged numbers and letters - are relatively easy to read for humans, with their similarity approach, but for computers this is virtually impossible because letters and numbers are so distorted that their systems cannot read them.

A computer needs commands to work step by step. *The brain acts on its own and creates new goals time and again, only by driving the survival and well-being of the living being.*

A computer almost never makes mistakes because it only calculates logically.

The brain can make many mistakes because it is creative and can draw wrong conclusions. The advantage, however, is the tremendous flexibility that makes it possible to use all the components and networks for specific goals. The downside is that it wants to explain everything and often does not look closely. The advantage is that it can produce results that often make sense from a nebulous occurrence from a few clues.

The computer always makes rational decisions - the brain can make irrational decisions that can make sense for each goal.

So, as you can see on closer inspection, they are two very different systems.

If one reads in general about the comparison brain - computer, then it is noticeable that time and again the speed is mentioned. This does not play the central role in the brain in this regard, but the link; That's the way man lives. And that does not create in this form and to this extent a computer - also not approximately.

People are always learning, forming new synapses and neural networks. Whenever someone has learned something, new synapses have formed or been amplified in his brain.

On the other hand, these are restricted or deleted when they are no longer used.

The individual synapses, which are available in billions of times, can each connect thousands of times with other synapses.

To reproduce all this into a computer, and let it act just like the brain, is hardly possible.

Conclusion: The brain is an organic tissue that wants to survive with humans and uses all the similarities in it. It makes its own interpretation, images and "truths". It always creates new aims.

The computer runs according to exactly predetermined steps.

Both are subject to precise but different laws. These are two completely different systems, each of which can only be described individually.

And a few more words about artificial intelligence (AI):

> **Intelligence means finding the most satisfactory solutions and answers to questions and problems. This usually involves a topic.**
>
> **Humans cannot have as comprehensive an intelligence as AI (in terms of the potentially huge amount of information stored), because the brain only has a limited cognitive memory and usually finds solutions through feelings.**

If you ask what pure intelligence is, the answer is: everything that is not accompanied by feelings.

This is alien to humans, because both sides (cognition and feelings) usually play a role in them.

The AI is supposed to suggest answers. To do this, it searches through all the data that could be part of the solution.

In this way, AI can give a satisfactory answer based on a precisely defined question.

And artificial intelligence (with its algorithms) answer questions that are sought in the stored information.

The brain (with its mind located within it for searching) and artificial intelligence (with its algorithms) answer questions that are sought in the stored information. As living tissue, the brain stores these primarily with feelings and cognitively. This is because life wants to preserve itself. And feelings (with regard to storage) have proven to be a space-saving option in the course of evolution.

AI, as a structure without feelings, does not have this aim; it only stores the information "cognitively". This allows it to answer questions that do not require sensory perceptions for answers (although it can of course add corresponding intelligent information about living beings that experience them).

The advantage over life is that feelings cannot distort the answers. For example, if answers do not fit for ethical reasons or personal views.

In general, when a person asks himself something, he not only receives cognitive answers from himself, but also emotional ones. These often take precedence and influence the result.

This is not the case with AI - of course it cannot, because it has no feelings.

If all information relating to a particular topic is stored and then the question arises as to how this can be used for a task and what suggestions there are, then AI has a clear advantage, as long as it does not involve emotions. Because it can store much more useful data and information than the brain, which usually also responds emotionally and thus possibly waters down the sober answer - but provides creative (emotional) answers.

And finally, a comparison of how living beings or artificial intelligence (AI) make statements:

- Life began about 3.5 billion years ago from matter - together with the emergence of feelings. With extensions, it still prefers to use them to make judgments today.

- Artificial intelligence forms answers from facts - uninfluenced by feelings.

Qualia problem

Qualia should therefore be understood as: The subjective experience of a spiritual – i.e. non-material state. And it is claimed: This can only be generated by the (likewise) non-material consciousness and not by the brain.

My Comment: Every mental state that we experience comes naturally from the (material) brain.

Qualia means value.

What is of great value
to people?

Especially the feelings!

So one can define qualia
as:

The perception of the
emotional value one
feels about an event or
thing.

Even today, people still believe in immaterial spirits. This belief found its way into metaphysics in antiquity. In modern times the name has been renamed ontology.
Of course, ghosts cannot be proved. And so people can create any number of myths with it.

This also includes the myth Qualia. This should show that humans are capable of immaterial sensations. This is relatively easy to disprove since all feelings come from the brain.

The mental (spiritual) states are located in the midpoints (neuron networks). They can be activated by sensors or aims, for example.

Everything we perceive first reaches the brain as sensory information. The brain then processes this information according to its purposes, including transforming it into a mental state (for comparison and potential modification), which then returns to consciousness. This is the source of our subjective experience. In other words, it is not consciousness that determines our view of the world, but the brain.

This is why different people often react differently to the same situation.

"Mental" means spiritual.
"Mind" means: The ability to jump from one network of neu-

rons (midpoint) to others in the brain at lightning speed in order to seek information regarding the aims.

> **A spirit, in the sense of an immaterial being, which our ancestors felt internally and then projected outwards, because the functioning of the brain - also with regard to the center mechanism - was completely unknown to them, only exists <u>in</u> humans.**
> **Everything else are projections that have no substance in reality.**
>
> **The "spirits" (i.e. the mental) in the human**

> **psyche are stimulated by aims to search for information and experiences. They can come into being and pass away, more or less playing along with and shaping people in the respective context with a certain value.**

The mental state is thus generated by information from the outside and inside world in the brain. Depending on the relevance, the consciousness (the sensors) that experiences this is then further activated.

This back and forth (brain> consciousness> brain> consciousness ...) could rock up more and more so that one is completely in the midpoints, for example the music can rise.

It is ignored by many (and therefore leads to a wrong view): The world is not the way we see it, but we perceive it as our aims (which are in the brain - more precisely: in the neural networks - they show us.

So, three reasons can be named that the Qualia problem proponents cannot perceive because they have other aims (for example not to allow materialism for life and to portray human beings as a being that spiritually surpasses everything - except for God or the like higher powers). They mean:

> 1. the world they see is the same for everyone,

> 2. They are not clear about the central role of aims

> 3. And they do not recognize the working methods and effects of the neural networks (midpoints).

People who say that there is a qualia problem that cannot be solved with a materialistic idea also have serious problems of understanding and explanation: They speak of consciousness and spirit, but cannot do either explain

convincingly - and accordingly not understand.

Again, and again the "argument"
comes up with them that no subjective
experience content can be explained
from matter.

This is wrong: In the beginning of life,
organic substances were created from
inorganic substances (both are of
course materialistic - and all organic
produce subjective experience content).

This is how organic substances came
about. These developed and created
new structures by means of evolution
towards the aim of life. Over time, the
brain in particular played an increasingly central role as a control system.

The difficulty lies particularly in the
fact that people do not want to admit
that consciousness is merely an amplification of the senses in order to
transmit information to the corresponding neural networks.

So, it is claimed that consciousness is
something quite extraordinary that

cannot be explained with physical and chemical principles.

To equate it merely with increased perception of the senses, which run on the fundamentals of physics and chemistry, is completely rejected because it does not fit into the picture that they have of consciousness in them.

Since i.a. these philosophers are shaped by their focus "metaphysics" (keywords: immortal soul, body-soul problem, free will, God, etc.), they are blind to the fact that one is with the brain, with whose physical and chemical fundamentals, mental subjective experiences and consciousness can certainly explain.

The midpoint "metaphysics" is the trap for their incomprehension.

It is like before with the Copernican system: The midpoint, the geocentric worldview - the earth is in the center of the universe - prevented the insight into the heliocentric worldview: The Earth is just a planet that moves around the sun. The leading intellectual class of that time could not and would not detach itself from this central focus within them, the geocentric worldview.

It only went out in the following generations.

The current view of consciousness is similar. This is not something that makes decisions and directs the brain, but it is controlled by the brain, which activates the consciousness accordingly through the respective information so that it can be experienced with strengthened senses and provides further information.

When one speaks of mental abilities, one actually means - often without being aware of it - the neural networks that have formed on the basis of aims. (They used to be unrecognizable. Today, computers can make them visible with the appropriate programs.) The more effectively and flexibly the midpoints interact with one another, the more mental abilities one has.

Again: "mind" because we cannot directly recognize the neural networks with our senses. They can be activated quickly and deactivated again just as quickly - like a ghost that appears and disappears again.

I would like to explain it again in terms of the musical experience: sensory impressions and stimuli are conveyed to the brain through perception. This activates the music midpoints stored in the brain. The brain qualifies the value of the sensory impressions according to its aims. People become aware of this through feelings, if the melody is an important aim for them, in order to experience the resulting feelings. The activated consciousness sends this information via the music to the brain, more precisely: to the corresponding midpoints (neural networks), which thereby generate increased feelings in the consciousness. This can build up more and more, so that one is completely absorbed in these midpoints. So, all other neural networks are more or less reduced in value.

To underpin the fact that music is found in the brain: there are musical and not so musical people. Where else than in the brain should this respective feeling or non-perception be genetically or epigenetically stored and take place?

Conclusion: Thus, the problem of qualia is merely a problem of perception for philosophers!

One more remark on the problem of intentionality in philosophy (i.e., the ability of humans to relate to something - for example to real or only imagined objects, properties or facts): If one assumes that consciousness and the SELF have mental states (outside, so to speak the brain's existing ghosts, immaterial), then you also have a problem.

This is based on statements by past philosophers who knew little about the functions of the brain. (If you don't know something, you often replace it with fantasies.)

But if one realistically assumes that these are states of the brain, then this problem does not exist.

Intentionality can therefore easily be explained with the aims in the brain.

Appendix:

Mary's room (thought experiment)

This is an example of the bizarre conclusions that a goal that must be achieved can lead the brain to. And it exemplifies the psychological complex (here a compulsive attitude that cannot be influenced or can only be influenced with great resistance).

The experiment is intended to prove that experience has a spiritual (immaterial) basis and cannot be explained solely with concrete scientific results (which are ultimately always material). The following scenario was conceived for this purpose:

The fictional super-scientist Mary has been locked in a laboratory where everything is painted in shades of grey since birth. So she's never seen colour before. At the same time, she is an outstanding physiologist who knows all the physical facts about seeing colours. However, when she is finally released from the lab, she learns what colours look like for the first time.

According to the author who came up with it, this is supposed to be proof that someone who perceives something for the first-time experiences it with their metaphysical mind.

Like everything in this field, which is now called ontology, this spirit is not explained (as is usual here in this discipline of philosophy.)

The question that the author posed at the heart of his proof of immaterial experience was: Did she learn something new about colour from this, even though she already knew all about it? If so, then the evidence for non-material experience would be established.

Since this experiment is still considered conclusive and still haunts certain minds, I would like to comment on it as follows:

Everyone has the ability to see colour (unless a genetic defect causes colour blindness). This natural aptitude is activated and experienced the moment colour comes into play. A basic learning of colours - in the sense of: "Wasn't there before" - does not take place.

Primordial structures

(Definition and Description)

> **After organismic units with the ability of structural self-preservation and self-reproduction had developed in the beginning of all life, primordial structures developed and were multiplied by evolution.**

The concept of the head, the leader, whom one trusts, has an essential part in the primordial structures. This was particularly important for living beings, such as prehistoric humans, in order to have aims, such as role models, in order to survive as best as possible.

Here is, with high probability, the actual cause from which the term "God" has formed.

Since this is deeply anchored in the nature of the person, the goal of subordinating himself to something, especially in the present, is shaped especially through feelings.

That there is something mystical, supernatural, God was an absolute truth for the primitive people, which conveyed their feelings to them. This has become embedded in the heritage.

Humans, as a rule, probably did not think about it because it was a fact for them.

In all people there are unconscious collective archetypes, ideas, patterns and schemes that work in them. (Even small children, for example, look for patterns and rules to understand the world). They are pictures or instructions of a form or behaviour that are deeply root-

ed in the human species and are inherited.

In particular to create survival and offspring. These have arisen through evolution (which, like everything, proceeds according to substances controlled by laws) - not through metaphysical powers.

Such as beauty, abhorrence of murder, fairness, Morality (in the sense of how one behaves towards others), pursuit of acceptance (recognition within a group), justice, freedom, autonomy, self-control, rejection of fraud / falseness.

If these patterns are not followed, feelings of vengeance and retribution can develop.

These can among other things to appear in a dream. These include also creating lives, producing offspring, growth, dating, the pursuit of a group, diffused notions of mystical beings (formed and anchored in phylogenesis, the phylogeny of human beings, fantasies experienced as realities).

On the latter: It is clear that mystical images, feelings, ideas, etc., have taken root in the genes of the primordial structures because the earlier humans could explain the world only through ghosts, gods, mysticism. All of us inherit this heritage through epigenetics.

In addition, there are, for example, patterns in the human being such as the pattern of the mother's breast or in the cat a scheme of the mouse.

These primordial structures are always only in the living beings - in the brain - , never outside, and, like everything in the universe, run according to laws.

Every genus has its image in it. Just as human has the image of people, or the recognition of gender types. In addition, there are also diffuse primal structures in the brain, such as a dwelling, flora and fauna, etc.

These primordial structures are important because you can build the environment faster, set vertices to better orient yourself.

Primordial structures are not concrete, but are formed according to the respective present. If they were specific - like the biological aims that have exact specifications in every human being - then the respective psychological aims would be too limited in their form. The images and ideas are therefore generally held and indistinct, because one must orientate each of the present, adapt. The clearer they would be, the closer the circle would be, the more difficult would be the adaptation. Just as memories rise in us, when we are confronted with similarities, so it is with the primordial structures, when midpoints are activated, which affect the archetypes.

So, as the body, the individual extremities, etc. are inherited, how they are to be designed exactly, so does the mental heredity. However, not exactly, but more than diffuse images and ideas, because otherwise, as I said, there is a risk that you cannot adapt to the present properly to achieve these aims to execute.

In the primordial ground of human there is e.g., the hero who is stimulated by a current sports hero or music hero and thus fired from the inside of the person - so that the (diffuse) image that one has within is fulfilled.

When you see a play or a movie, read a book that pleases you, if you want to know yourself, you can ask why you like it. One will always encounter primordial structures that lie in one, are thus stimulated and brought to life by them.

The effect of the primordial structures could be imagined on the example of an artist: he has a kind of picture - an idea - in himself, which he cannot recognize at first but creates his works towards this aim.

The vague image of a god in one, who stands for security and support, is also an archetype that takes shape in reference persons, such as parents.

Here is also the desire for a saviour.

▶ **Complex to follow someone**: the devotion to someone who has been assigned special abilities and whom one trusts to the point of blindness.

So, once the thought of God or an overpowering power in one occurs (which is not so rare) that they have caused something, then it should be remembered that this came from a self, from its own primordial structure.

That it does not come from the outside, but from the inside.

In humans, the archetype seems to exist, to subordinate something (vital). For example, the baby of his mother, the child of his parents. This is about life, protection and security.

There is often a leader in the adult world.
Here is also the explanation why the family in particular is of such great value for the individual: here one feels cared for and supported.
This is then extended to the partnership as an important step, the wider environment; etc. local community,

society, associations, the people in which one lives.

As I said: All listed aims or midpoints of the primal structures run mostly unconsciously and shape the human being. And all are substances that run according to laws.

Here are the main reasons for the drives, the behaviour of the people.

As already mentioned, the most important are to survive and to produce offspring.

►The first I call the life complex: So, the trigger to live as long as you can, regardless of the circumstances.

► The second I call the offspring complex: So, the mainspring to produce offspring, regardless of the environmental conditions.

By activating the primal structures, the deeper psyche of the human being can be reached, also in order to possibly act on it.

The key to this is simple stories, fairy tales, pictorial illustrations, etc.

One more word about the archetypes (as defined by C.G. Jung): ancient commonalities which lie deep in the hereditary mass and of which people are shaped by unconscious patterns of thought and action.

Epilogue

> **Finally, I would like to remind you in particular of these three natural foundations by which we are shaped (willingly or not):**

1. Deep drives in every human being

▶ **Life-complex**: To live as long as you can, regardless of the circumstances.

▶ **Producer-complex**: The mainspring to produce offspring, regardless of the environmental conditions.

▶ **Complex to follow someone**: the devotion to someone who is assigned special abilities and who is trusted to the point of blindness.

2. God

From the last (**Complex to follow someone**), there is, with high probability, the actual cause from which the term "<u>God</u>" was formed.

As a rule, it is difficult to escape the feelings that have formed and embedded in the psyche from the beginning of the multicellular life to the present.

It would be helpful to use human cognitive abilities; But even with this, these feelings are often difficult to influence.

3. Naturally predetermined

That everything had to come the way it came is documented from two sides:

▶Identic parts under identical circumstances <u>always</u> result in identical structures.

▶The statistical calculation of probability enables mathematicians to make very precise predictions about quantum systems. This would not be feasible if there was lawlessness here.

And something else essential:

It is often forgotten that people are only living beings that developed from inorganic substances and, like these, are shaped by laws. The main difference between inorganic and organic substances is **the aim of survival.**

The main difference between humans and other living beings is their brain, which is capable of forming exorbitant neural networks, with which they can recognize laws and create new processes.

And - with which an infinite number of imaginative structures can be fooled into him.

Let me add a few basic words about the relationship between my (potential) readers and me:

People are guided by aims. These can and are influenced by the midpoint mechanics. In such a way that what speaks against them is perceived less or not at all.

As a rule, you don't notice anything about these processes because they are part of the routine that the brain carries out on a daily basis.

This influence applies to a relatively large part of my representations, because I am not concerned with serving the images and expectations of others, but rather writing what I have learned through my research.

Like: To me, consciousness is what one perceives with heightened senses - and not how one likes to see it; as a property of our brains by which we know everything about him.

Constructive criticism was and still is particularly helpful to me.

Other books by me:

- Blindheit der Klugen
- Blindness of the wise
- Mittelpunkt der Psyche
- Midpoint of the psyche
- Die Entzauberung des Bewusstseins (geänderte Auflage)
- Was Gläubige wissen sollten
- What Believers Should Know
- Die Nicht-Entstehung des Universums
- The non-creation of the universe
- Wutgefühle: (Wie Gefühle entstanden und den Menschen bewegen)
- Feelings of anger: (How feelings arose and move people)
- Die Welt ohne Metaphysik: (Eine klare Sicht auf den Menschen und die Welt)
- The world without metaphysics: (A clear view of human and the world)
- 3 Gründe: Psychologische Grundlagen des Menschen ●●● Physikalische Grundlagen der Welt ●●● Betrachtungen des Glaubens
- 3 Basics of human beings